George Clinch

Antiquarian Jottings

Relating to Bromley, Hayes Keston, and West Wickham, in Kent

George Clinch

Antiquarian Jottings
Relating to Bromley, Hayes Keston, and West Wickham, in Kent

ISBN/EAN: 9783337142711

Printed in Europe, USA, Canada, Australia, Japan

Cover: Foto ©ninafisch / pixelio.de

More available books at **www.hansebooks.com**

Antiquarian Jottings

RELATING TO

Bromley, Hayes, Keston, and West Wickham, in Kent.

BY

GEORGE CLINCH,
OF THE DEPARTMENT OF PRINTED BOOKS, BRITISH MUSEUM.

OLD MARKET HOUSE, BROMLEY, KENT.

Printed for the Author, Addiscombe, Surrey,
by Messrs Turnbull & Spears, Edinburgh.

1889.

CONTENTS.

	PAGE
BROMLEY	3
THE MANOR OF BROMLEY	5
BROMLEY PALACE	10
ST BLAZE'S WELL	24
SIMPSON'S PLACE	28
THE MANOR OF SUNDRIDGE	33
BLACKBROOK	35
BROMLEY HILL PLACE	38
BROMLEY COLLEGE	43
BROMLEY CHURCH	55
EASTER SEPULCHRE	60
PARISH CHURCH GOODS	62
CHURCH PLATE	65
BELLS	67
CHURCH DOOR	70
BRASSES	71
MONUMENTS	74
BENEFACTIONS	80
PARISH REGISTERS	81
RECTORS AND VICARS	83
THE RECTORY	85
PARISH UMBRELLA	86

CONTENTS.

	PAGE
BROMLEY—*continued.*	
Funereal Garland	86
Ravenscroft	90
The "Bull Inn"	90
Bromley Tokens	91
Proclamation of James II.	91
Old Market House	92
Widmore	93
HAYES	97
Hayes Church	97
Brasses	100
Monuments	103
Parish Church Goods	107
Parish Register	110
Hayes Place	115
Pickhurst Manor	119
Baston Manor	119
Pit Dwellings at Hayes Common	122
Ancient Earthworks at Toots Wood	126
Jacob's Well	129
KESTON	133
Windmills	133
The Archdeacon's Well	134
Cæsar's Well	135
Holwood Camp	136
Holwood House	139
Ancient Trees	141

CONTENTS. vii

	PAGE
KESTON—*continued*.	
KESTON CHURCH	142
PARISH CHURCH GOODS	145
BELLS	145
MONUMENTAL INSCRIPTIONS	147
WAR BANK	150
WEST WICKHAM	157
PARISH CHURCH	157
MONUMENTS (AND BRASSES)	160
ROODSCREEN	165
BELLS	166
PAINTED GLASS	167
PARISH CHURCH GOODS	170
CHARITIES	172
PARISH REGISTER	172
LICH GATE	173
WEST WICKHAM COURT	173
EARTHWORKS	178
FLINT IMPLEMENTS	180
ANCIENT EXCAVATIONS	187
INDEX	189

ILLUSTRATIONS.

Bromley Church	*Frontispiece*
Old Market House, Bromley	*Vignette on Title-Page*
	PAGE
St Blaze's Well	28
Simpson's Place	32
Hayes Place	118
Norman Carving, Keston Church	143
Funereal Urn, War Bank	151
West Wickham Church (Exterior)	158
West Wickham Church (Interior)	164
Ovoid Flint (Palæolithic)	184
Javelin-head (Neolithic)	185
Wrought Flints	186

BROMLEY.

A

BROMLEY.

The name Bromley, anciently written, in English, Bromleag and Bromleah, and, in Latin, Bromlega, appears to have originated from the common broom, which formerly grew here in great abundance. The name therefore signifies a field or pasture where broom grows.

Bromley Parish is bounded by no less than eight others. It contains about three thousand acres of land, of which three hundred and fifty were coppice wood, and two hundred and fifty waste land, in 1798. Formerly there was much more woodland, nearly a third of the parish having been so occupied about the middle of the seventeenth century.

Of Bromley in prehistoric times not many traces remain, but a few neolithic implements have been found there from time to time. Mr Cecil Brent, F.S.A., has found, in Sundridge Park, a well-made flint celt, 3¾ inches in length, of neolithic date, which has been first neatly shaped by chipping, and afterwards finished by grinding. The same gentleman possesses a British urn of red clay, which was found in Elmfield Road. A few coins have been found in Bromley, but they have been pronounced to be of doubtful authenticity. One, a silver denarius of Antoninus Pius, which was found near Bromley Cemetery, did not appear to have been long buried. Mr George H. Payne, to whom I am indebted for the information, tells me it was probably lost (for the second time, perhaps) in the nineteenth century.

In the year 1864 a very interesting discovery of pottery was made at Beechfield, the residence of Mr James W. Ilott. A workman employed in making some alterations of the grounds, turned up, from a depth of about fourteen or sixteen inches below the surface, a sepulchral vase of coarse red ware, ornamented with oblique longitudinal lines. By the side of the vase was about a shovelful of bones and fragments of tile. The vase itself was completely filled with a quantity of bones, partially incinerated, some of which Mr Ilott pronounced to be human. Further search revealed two vessels in an upright position, and fragments of about six or eight others, among which was a fragment of fine red Samian ware, decorated with two parallel bands. Among them were one vessel of Roman Salopian ware, with narrow neck and handle, and one of bluish-black Upchurch ware. There were also some rusty iron nails. Some particulars of this discovery were published in the *Bromley Record* of June 1864. There can be no doubt that these relics mark the site of a Romano-British burial-ground. The incinerated human bones, collected and carefully placed in the urn, are a clear and decisive indication of the custom of cremation which we know was common amongst the Romans, and of which many remains have been found in connection with Roman antiquities all over this country. It is an especially interesting fact to us, as a proof that this particular spot was inhabited by the Romans.

A few fragments of Norman pottery were found among the old foundations when the new chancel was added to the Parish Church.

A very curious funereal garland, in gold and silver filigree work, found in 1733 in the churchyard, will be particularly referred to in the body of this volume.

THE MANOR OF BROMLEY.

"Ethelbert, King of Kent, gave to Bishop Eardulph and the church of Rochester, land in Bromley, containing six sulings.[1]

"King Edgar, in the ninth year of his reign, anno 967,[2] granted to St Andrew, and the church of Rochester, certain land at the place, commonly known by the name of *Æt Bromlcage*, containing ten hides, called by the Kentishmen, *sulings*, with all liberties and emoluments whatsoever; excepting the repelling invasions, and the repairing of bridges and fortifications,[3] which privileges were granted on account of the great price which Bishop Alfstan had paid for this land; being no less than eighty marcs of the purest gold, and six pounds of fine silver, and thirty marcs of gold besides to the king's *præfect*.

"At the end of this grant is a list of the several woods or denberries in Andredreswald, or the Weald, the commodity of which belonged to this land of Bromley. Part of this land might probably be the same which was given before by King Ethelbert; for in the donations of the Saxon kings, the same manors and estates are frequently recorded as having been given by different kings, which happened by their dissensions and contentions with each other, with

---

[1] "Suling," a word peculiar to Kent. It is supposed to mean the same as carucate, but here it seems to be of greater extent. In some parts of Domesday a suling is described as containing about 220 acres.—*Lysons*.

[2] The date of this charter in the *Textus Roffensis* is misprinted, viz., in the 9th year of king Edgar, anno 955; for that king did not begin his reign till 959; and *Dunstan*, who, as one of the witnesses, signs himself *Abp. of Canterbury*, did not come to that see till the year 960.

[3] This was an exception in all the Saxon grants of lands made to the Church in this country.

various success, and one while taking away the possessions of the church, and another while regranting them again. Besides, it is to be observed, that when different kings have given small parcels of land in the same parish or manor, as appears by many instances in the Saxon codicils, they have been said to have given the whole of such parish or manor, instead of such small part of it.

"King Ethelred, son of Edgar, on some dispute with the bishop of Rochester, laid waste the lands belonging to his see, and in 987 gave to his minister, Æthelsine (by whose advice he had taken several estates from it), ten plow lands at Bromley.

"But afterwards, he, with much contrition, in 998, in the presence of the convent of Rochester, and his principal nobility, declared what he had done was by the advice of this Æthelsine; and then restored to the church six plow lands here, together with the privilege of the woods in the Weald, etc.

"One Birtrick, a Saxon nobleman, and Elfswithe, his wife, of Meopham, in this county, bequeathed by their testament, made in the time of Alfstan, bishop of Rochester, who died in 984, their land at Bromley, after Britware's life, to St Andrew's Priory, in Rochester, as Elfric their lord had bequeathed it for him and his ancestors.

"After the Conquest, Odo, the great bishop of Baieux, the king's half-brother, seized on the possessions of the church of Rochester, at Bromley, among many other estates belonging to it; but Archbishop Lanfranc did not suffer him to keep them long, for he recovered them, in the solemn assembly of the whole county, held on this occasion, by the king's command, at Pinenden-heath, in 1076, and afterwards restored them to Bishop Gundulph, and the church of St Andrew; which donation was confirmed by Archbishop Anselm, and several of his successors. In the reign of King Edward the Confessor, Bromley continued to be estimated at six sulings. Whether the whole of them came into the hands of the bishop of Baieux, I do not find; but it is certain only three of them returned after the above adjudication to the church of Rochester.

"Accordingly this estate is thus entered, under the general title of the bishop of Rochester's lands, in the survey of Domesday, taken in the year 1080.

"*In Bromlei hundred the same bishop (of Rochester) holds Bromlei. It was taxed at six sulings in the time of King Edward the Confessor, and now at three. The arable land is 13 carucates. In demesne there are two carucates, and 30 villeins, with 26 borderers, having 11 carucates. There is one mill of four shillings, and two acres of meadow. Wood for the pannage of 100 hogs. In the time of king Edward the Confessor, and afterwards, it was worth 12 pounds and 10 shillings, now 18 pounds, and yet it yields 21 pounds, all but two shillings.*" (Hasted's "History of Kent.")

At this point it will be well to turn to an admirable sketch of "The Church and Manor of Bromley," by Mr W. T. Beeby, M.D., which was read at the Congress of the Kent Archæological Society, at Bromley, in July 1878, and subsequently printed in the proceedings of that Society (*Archæologia Cantiana, vol. xiii.*) Dr Beeby, speaking of the Manor of Bromley, says, "It was a poor manor, neither pasture nor arable land being worth much, and hence, soon after the Conquest, portions of it were converted into knight's fees; and while, at the time of Domesday survey, there is no mention of any owners of land in Bromley besides the Bishop of Rochester, shortly after this date there were several freeholders in the place.

"It seems probable that the practice of sub-infeudation by lords of manors had become general before the reign of John, inasmuch as he granted a charter with permission to the Archbishops of Canterbury to convert into knights' fees any lands of the fee of their church held in gavelkind.

"Concerning the sub-infeudation and various other matters, I am indebted to information received from the late Coles Child, Esq., owner of Bromley Manor, who kindly allowed me access to his manuscript notes.

"He says, 'There can be little doubt that the Bishops of Rochester, either with or without direct permission from the crown, had converted portions of their lands in Bromley, and elsewhere, into knights' fees, in like manner as the Archbishops had been authorised to do.'

"In less than a century after the Domesday survey, twenty-seven persons held of the Bishop by military service."

It is very probable that the estate or manor known as Simpsons, was one of the earliest estates which was severed from the original manor, but of this it will be more convenient to treat when we come to consider Simpsons Place. Two other manors, Sundridge and Blakebrok, or Blackbrook, were subsequently instituted. The latter manor was situated somewhere near Southborough.

Returning now to the Bishop's manor we may note that in the 21st year of King Edward I., Thomas de Woldham, Bishop of Rochester, claimed certain liberties, viz., the return of the king's writs, assize of bread and ale,[1] view of frank-pledge,[2] and pleas of

---

[1] The assize of bread and ale, whereby the size, weight, or dimensions of certain commodities were regulated. The Statute of Bread and Ale, 51 Hen. III.

[2] Frane-pledge. A pledge or surety for the behaviour of a freeman: called also Fribargh.

withernam,[1] in his manor of Bromley, as well of his own tenants, as those of the parson of that parish; and he complained, that Abel de St. Martin, parson of Bromley, caused, in like manner, amerciaments to be levied of the tenants of his church, when it happened they were amerced at the Bishop's view of Bromley for breaking the assize. Notwithstanding which, the Bishop causing the same to be levied by his bailiffs too, the tenants were twice punished for the same default; whereupon the jury found upon oath, that the Bishop had a right to those liberties, and that he found his church possessed of them upon his coming to it. Upon which the parson submitted, and was fined half a marc.

"Anno 14 king Edward II., (1320), Bishop Hamo de Heth was necessitated to sell the wood of Elmsted in Bromley, which he did for two hundred marcs, to pay the debts which his church had incurred in soliciting the affairs of it at Rome. In the 25th and 26th years of king Henry VI. the Bishop of Rochester had a most ample confirmation of all former charters and liberties, and a grant of a market in his manor of Bromley, on a Thursday weekly, and one fair in the village here, on the feast of St. James the Apostle, and another within this manor, on the day of St. Blaze," (*Registrum Roffense*.) These fairs have, since the alteration of the calendar, been held on 5th August, and 14th February. The fairs, with the market and market-house, were let on lease by the Bishops of Rochester, the last lease expiring in 1862. But the fairs having become a great annoyance to the inhabitants, the late Lord of the Manor took steps to put them down.

[1] Withernam. A taking or reprisal of other cattle or goods, in lieu of those that were formerly unjustly taken or eloigned, or otherwise withholden: it signifies also reprisals taken at sea by letters of mark.

The Manor appears to have remained in the possession of the Bishops of Rochester up till the time of the great rebellion, when the parliament passed an ordinance, October 9, 1646, for the abolition of archbishops and bishops, and for vesting their land and possessions in trustees, to be disposed of according to the appointment of both houses; and another (Nov. 16) for the sale of them, to satisfy the debts due from the state upon the public faith. In consequence of which the manor of Bromley, with its appurtenances, as part possessions of the bishopric of Rochester, was sold in 1648, to Augustine Skinner, for £5665 11s. 11d., in which situation it remained till the restoration of King Charles II. in 1660, when it returned again, with the palace, to its right and lawful owner in the person of Dr. John Warner, Bishop of Rochester. It remained in the possession of the Bishops of Rochester until the year 1845, when it was sold by virtue of an Act of Parliament. Coles Child, Esq., the father of the present lord of the manor was the purchaser.

Bromley Palace.

Hasted is of opinion that a mansion or palace was erected at Bromley by Bishop Gundulph soon after the year 1080, and that it was but a mean and inconvenient habitation; "at least (says he) it was in the time of Bishop Gualeranus, who died in 1184, become so ruinous, that his successor, Bishop Gilbert de Glanvill, found it necessary to rebuild it in a more commodious manner." The same reason which led Hasted to suppose the building a mean one, *i.e.*, the speedy decay of the fabric, has led Dr. W. T. Beeby to form the opinion that it probably was not the work of Bishop Gundulph at all, all that prelate's known buildings being of a massive and enduring character. It may be doubted whether walls of great solidity and strength would have been necessary for the bishop's palace at Bromley, which at that early date was probably of humble dimensions. From Dr. Beeby's paper on "The Church and Manor of Bromley," (already referred to), we take the liberty of making the following extract: "The first house and gardens probably did not cover a larger space than two acres, and were surrounded by a moat. The masonry supporting the ancient drawbridge, the remains of which consisted of a rude mass of flint and chalk, cemented together by mortar which had become as hard as stone, were discovered by Mr Child some years since, about forty-five yards north of the present house; and it was then impossible to open the ground to the south without meeting with foundation walls, the lower portions of which were constructed of blocks of chalk."

Roger Forde, abbot of Glastonbury, a man of great learning and eloquence, was killed at this palace, in the time of Bishop Laurence de St. Martin, on a journey which he undertook to defend the rights of his church, in the year 1261.

The palace has had many additions made to it from time to time. Among its benefactors we may reckon Bishop Sprat (1684-1713), who, by a license granted by the Archbishop of Canterbury in 1669, pulled down and rebuilt the Chapel, and much improved the grounds about it. (To the malignant plot against Bishop Sprat we shall have occasion to allude later on.) The license gave authority to "demolish and take away" the old "chappell," which was "wainscotted eight foote high with oake wainscott," and ornamented with "old fashioned small panels." This chapel adjoined the gatehouse and was separate from the mansion, a room within which was proposed as a substitute for the old chapel, and on October 30th, 1701, it was consecrated. Bishop Atterbury the next bishop of Rochester made some expensive additions to the palace. But the greatest benefactor to it was Bishop Wilcocks, whose reparations of the buildings, and improvements of the gardens and grounds about the house, were executed with no small cost and elegance. After that time it remained with little alteration until 1774, in which year Dr. John Thomas, the newly appointed Bishop of Rochester, finding the house much dilapidated, pulled the whole of it down, and built the present palace, which bears the date 1775, and the arms of the bishop quartered with those of his see. The building was completed in 1776.

The folio edition of Hasted's History of Kent (vol. i. p. 90), contains a large engraving of the ancient episcopal palace at Bromley, taken before the year 1756, wherein the gable of the old chapel is shown to have been surmounted by a globular stone ornament, and similar stones are represented upon the tops of two small pinnacles, which flank it. Some ornamental water, outbuildings, and a view of the grounds and timber of the surrounding park, are comprised in the picture. In the foreground are representations of Bishop Wilcocks, a lady, and perhaps a servant to whom the bishop appears to be giving some directions.

"I am not aware that any objects of interest have been found during the various alterations effected of late years in the manorial property, with the exception of the leather sole of a shoe with pointed toe, such as were worn in the middle ages, and some broken glass of some wine flasks." (Dr. Beeby, *Archæol. Cant.*, vol. xiii., p. 156.)

BISHOPS OF ROCHESTER WHO HAVE LIVED AT BROMLEY PALACE.

JOHN WARNER. This prelate was the son of Herman Warner, a citizen of London, and was born in 1585. At Magdalen College, Oxford, he took his degree of B.A. in 1602. In 1614 he was presented to the rectory of St Michael's, Crooked Lane, which he resigned in 1616. In 1625 he became rector of St Dionis Backchurch, in Fenchurch Street. Later on he was collated by the Archbishop of Canterbury (Abbot) to the prebend of the first stall in the Cathedral of Canterbury. He was also appointed Governor of Sion College, London, and was made chaplain to Charles I. In 1633 he became Dean of Lichfield, and, in 1637, Bishop of Rochester. He is said to have been an accurate logician and philosopher, and well versed in the fathers and schoolmen. He was a man of decided and cheerful character. To his munificence Bromley owes the very excellent institution known as Bromley College, although in fact it is a home for the residence and maintenance of the widows of clergymen. Bishop Warner died in 1666, and was buried in Rochester Cathedral, where a handsome monument was erected to his memory in the small chapel at the east end of the north aisle.

In 1645, Warner published a little duodecimo volume, entitled "The Gayne of Losse, or Temporal Losses Spiritually Improved. In a Centurye & One Decad of Meditations & Resolves" (pp. xvi. 162), and also two tracts:

"Church-lands not to be Sold, or, A Necessary and Plaine Answer to the Question of a Conscientious Protestant: *Whether the Lands of the Bishops and Churches in England and Wales may be Sold?*" 4to, 1648 (pp. 81.)

"The Devilish Conspiracy, Hellish Treason, Heathenish Condemnation, and Damnable Murder, Committed, and Executed by the Jews against the Anointed of the Lord, Christ their King. . . . As it was delivered in a Sermon on the 4th February, 1648." . . . 4to, London, 1648 (pp. 45.)

JOHN DOLBEN. Bishop Warner was succeeded by Bishop John Dolben, a man of considerable worth, abilities, and eminence. He was born at Stanwick, in Northamptonshire, in 1625, and was educated at Westminster School, where he was admitted a king's scholar in 1636. In 1640 he was elected to Christ Church, Oxford, where he was admitted a student on Queen Elizabeth's foundation. When the civil wars broke out, Mr Dolben took arms for the royal cause in the garrison at Oxford, and served as an ensign in the unfortunate battle of Marston-Moor, in 1644, where he received a gunshot wound of a serious nature in the shoulder; but in the defence of York, soon after, he received a severer wound in the thigh, which broke the bone, and confined him twelve months to his bed. In 1646 Dolben returned to his college and renewed his studies, and in 1656 he took holy orders. In 1660 the king, restored " to his own again," did not forget Dolben's services. He was appointed a canon of Christ Church, Oxford. After many preferments and honours, which were bestowed upon him with great rapidity, he was consecrated Bishop of Rochester in 1666, and was allowed to hold the Deanery of Westminster *in commendam*. He was translated to the See of York in 1683, and in 1686, after a life of singular vicissitude, he died. He was buried in the Minster at York, where is a handsome monument with an inscription recording his merits and the principal circumstances of his life. As an author not much remains to testify his abilities, although it is said his sermons well deserved publication. Three sermons preached before the king were printed.

FRANCIS TURNER, Bishop of Rochester, 1683-4.

THOMAS SPRAT, a learned English prelate, was born in 1636, at Tallaton in Devonshire, the son of a clergyman, and having been educated at a little school by the churchyard side, became a Commoner of Wadham College, Oxford, in 1651. In 1684 he was made Bishop of Rochester, holding *in commendam* the Deanery of Westminster, owing to the smallness of the revenue of the See of Rochester. In 1692 a strange and malignant attack was made upon him by two men named Robert Young and Stephen Blackhead, both men convicted of infamous crimes, and both, when the scheme was laid, prisoners in Newgate. Sprat published an account of the plot in a book entitled " A Relation of the Late Wicked Contrivance of Stephen Blackhead and Robert Young, against the Lives of several Persons, by Forging an *Association* under their Hands. Written by the Bishop of *Rochester*. *In Two Parts:* The First Part being a Relation of what passed at the Three Examinations of the said Bishop by a Committee of the Lords of the *Privy-Council.* The Second being an Account of the Two above-mentioned authors of the Forgery. *In the* Savoy: Printed by Edward Jones. MDCXCII." 4to. (pp. 1-75, i.-vi., 1-164.) The relation is written in a readable style, and, as the book is rather rare, a few extracts from it may be not altogether devoid of interest.

"It was on *Saturday,* the seventh of *May* of this present year, 1692, in the Evening, as I was walking in the Orchard at *Bromley,* Meditating on something I design'd to Preach the next Day ; that I saw a Coach and four Horses stop at the outer Gate, out of which two Persons alighted. Immediately I went towards them, believing they were some of my Friends, coming to give me a Visit. By that time I was got to the Gate, they were enter'd into the Hall: But seeing me hastning to them, they turn'd, and met me about the middle of the Court. The Chief of them perceiving me to look wistly on them, as being altogether Strangers to me, said *My Lord. Perhaps you do not know me. My name is* Dyve, *I am Clerk of the Council, and here is one of the King's Messengers. I am sorry I am sent on this Errand. But I am come to Arrest you upon suspicion of High Treason.*

"Sir, said I, I suppose you have a Warrant for so doing; I pray let me see it. He shew'd it me. I read it; and the first Name I lighted on being the Earl of *Nottingham*'s; I said, Sir, I believe this is my Lord *Nottingham*'s own Hand, and I submit. What are your Orders how to dispose of me? *My Lord*, said he, *I must first search your Person, and demand the Keys you have about you.* My Keys I presently gave him. He search'd my Pockets; and found no Papers, but some poor Notes of a Sermon, and a letter from Mr *B. Fairfax* about ordinary Business.

"*Now*, says he, *My Lord, I must require to see the Rooms to which these Keys belong, and all the Places in the House, where you have any Papers or Books.* I straight conducted him up Stairs into my Study. This, Sir, said I, is the only Chamber where I keep all the Books and Papers I have in the House. They began to Search, and with great readiness turn'd over everything in the Room, and Closets, and Presses, shaking every Book by the Cover, opening every part of a Chest of Drawers, where were many Papers, particularly some Bundles of Sermons; which I told them were my proper Tools; and that all that knew me, could Vouch for

me, it was not my custom to have any Treason in them. . . .
Then they went into my Bedchamber, and the Closets adjoining,
doing as they had done in my Study, feeling about the Bed, and
Hangings, and Knocking the Wainscot in several places, to see if
there were any private Hole, or Secret Conveyance.

"After that they came down Stairs, and search'd the Parlour
and Drawing-Room on that side of the House with the like exact-
ness. In all these Rooms I observed they very carefully pryed
into every part of the Chimneys; the Messenger putting his Hand
into every Flower-Pot: Which I then somewhat smiled at: But
since I found he had but too much Reason so to do.

"When they had done searching in all those Rooms, and in the
Hall as they were going out, and had taken with them what Papers
they thought fit; they carryed Me away in the Coach that brought
them. . . . . And so, between Ten and Eleven at Night,
we arrived at *Whitehal*, and I was brought to my Lord *Nottingham*,
whom I found alone in his Office."

"My Lord, said I, I am come upon your Warrant; but certainly
there must be some great Mistake, or black Villany in this Business.
For I declare, as in the Presence of God, I am absolutely free from
any just Accusation relating to the Government. His Lordship
told me, *He himself was much surprized when he heard my Name
mentioned*. I intreated him I might be Examined that Night, if
any Witnesses could be produced against me. He said, *That
could not possibly be, because the Lords, who had the Management of
such Affairs, were separated and gone Home: But that I was to
appear before them the next Day; and in the mean time, all the
Civility should be shown me, that could be expected by a Man in my
Condition.*

"My Lord, said, I, I hope, it being so very late, you will suffer me to lie at my own House at *Westminster*. He reply'd, *You shall do so; But you must have a Guard of Soldiers and a Messenger with you.* A Guard of Soldiers said I, My Lord, methinks is not so necessary to secure one of my Profession; I should rather offer, that I may have two or more Messengers to keep me, tho' that may put me to greater Charges. My Lord, said he, *I, for my own part, would be glad, if I might take your Parole; But I must do what I may answer to others; and therefore I pray be Content.*

"At this I acquiesced; only adding, My Lord, here are divers Papers brought up with me, which, upon my Credit, are but of common Importance; yet, because they are most of them private Talk among Friends; there may be some Expressions, which no Man if it were his own Case, would be willing to have divulg'd; and for, I desire your Lordship will take Care they may not be shewn to the Prejudice of any. He answer'd, *you have to do with Men of Honour: And you shall have no Occasion to complain upon that Account.*

"And so I was convey'd home to *Westminster* by Mr *Dyve*, and Mr *Knight* the Messenger, in the Coach with Me, and a Guard attending on each side. After we came to the Deanery, Mr *Dyve* having diligently surveyed my Lodgings, and the Avenues to them, left Me about Mid-night, with a strict Charge to the Messenger and Soldiers, not to give me any unnecessary Disturbance; but to watch carefully at my Bed-Chamber-Door till further Orders, which they did.

"The next Day, being *Sunday*, *May* the 8th, Mr *Dyve* came again to me about Noon, to acquaint me, That I was to attend the Committee of the Council that Evening by Six o'the Clock. And, says he, *My Lord, I suppose you have here also at* Westminster *a Room where you keep the rest of your Books and Papers.* I told him, I had. *Then*, said he, *I have Commission to search there likewise; particularly in your Cabinet.* I shewed him my Library, and gave him the Keys. He opened all the Presses of Books, and viewed particularly every Shelf, and examined every Drawer in the Cabinet: But finding nothing there of a late date, or that might afford any the least shadow of a Trayterous Correspondence, he went away without removing any one Paper thence.

"At the time appointed I was brought by the Messenger and Guard to *Whitehal*, where a select Number of the Lords of the Council were assembled at my Lord *Nottingham*'s Lodgings. There were present, as I remember, the Earl of *Devonshire* Lord Steward, the Earl of *Dorset* Lord Chamberlain, the Earl of *Nottingham* Secretary of State, the Earl of *Rochester*, the Earl of *Portland*, the Lord *Sydney* Lord Lieutenant of Ireland, and Sir *Edward Seymor*."

Then follow the questions put and bishop's answers to them, but they are too lengthy for reproduction here. Bishop Sprat remained in confinement until the 18th of May, when he addressed a letter to the Earl of Nottingham asking for his liberty on the ground of his innocence and impaired health.

"This Letter was read in the Cabinet Council that Day, and it had the Desired Effect; for thereupon I was ordered to be discharged that Evening; which accordingly was done about ten at Night, by Mr *Shorter*, a Messenger of the Chamber, coming to my House, and dismissing the Messenger, and taking off the Guard.

"The next Morning, being *May* 19th, to prevent any Concourse or Congratulations usual upon such Occasions, I retired early to

Bromley, where I remained quiet till *June* the 9th, little dreaming of a worse Mischief still hanging over my head."

The Bishop was, on June the 10th and 13th, examined again before the Privy Council, and confronted with his accusers. Young persisted with great impudence against the strongest evidence; but the resolution of Blackhead gradually gave way. He confessed, when closely questioned, that he left the paper in the flower-pot in the Bishop's chimney, upon the instigation of Robert Young. At length no doubt remained of the Bishop's innocence, and he was acquitted. His gratitude for the happy issue was so great that he commemorated it through life by a day of yearly thanksgiving. After this the Bishop passed his days in the quiet exercise of his functions. He lived to his seventy-ninth year, and died May 20, 1713. An elaborate marble monument in the south aisle of Westminster Abbey commemorates him. He wrote "The History of the Royal Society of London," 4to, London, 1667, and he published "An Account of the Life and Writings of A. Cowley," fol., London, 1669, and some translations and sermons. According to Spence, in his Anecdotes, Pope used to call Sprat "a worse Cowley."

FRANCIS ATTERBURY. This elegant scholar and ambitious churchman was born on the 6th of March 1662, at his father's rectory at Milton-Keynes, near Newport-Pagnel, in Buckinghamshire. He was educated at Westminster School, from whence he was removed, in 1680, to Christ Church College, Oxford, where he was indefatigable in his pursuit after knowledge, and very shortly distinguished himself by his classical attainments. In 1684 Atterbury took his degree of Bachelor of Arts, and in 1687 that of Master of Arts. On the accession of Queen Anne, Atterbury, who had entered the church, was appointed one of the queen's chaplains;

in October 1704, he was raised to the Deanery of Carlisle; in
1712 he was appointed Dean of Christ Church, and in June, the
following year, was advanced to the Deanery of Westminster and
Bishopric of Rochester. He was much given to controversy, and
he was the friend of the wits of his day. He was the intimate
companion of Pope, Bolingbroke, Swift, and Gay.

The death of Queen Anne, and the accession of George the
First to the throne, proved a death-blow to the ambitious hopes of
Atterbury. He was well known to be attached to the exiled
House of Stuart, and, consequently, his dangerous principles and
high rank in the church, rendered him peculiarly an object of
dislike and distrust. His disaffection, indeed, is said to have proceeded to such lengths, that, on the death of Queen Anne, when
statesmen and soldiers alike held back for fear of consequences, the
churchman was the only adherent of the exiled family who boldly
proposed to proclaim the Pretender as the King of England. The
neglect which he encountered from the King and his ministry,
tended not a little to increase his disaffection to the government.
Accordingly, when,—on the landing of the Pretender in Scotland
in 1715,—the Archbishop of Canterbury called on the Bishops in
and near London to testify their abhorrence of the Rebellion,
Atterbury boldly opposed himself to the wishes of the Primate,
and refused to sign the Declaration of the Bishops, of their
attachment to the crown. The ministry obtained information of
his being engaged in a plot in favour of the Pretender, and caused
him to be apprehended on the charge of high treason. He was
seated in his dressing-gown in the Deanery of Westminster, when
the Under-Secretary of State, accompanied by one of the messengers
of his office, suddenly entered his apartment, and declared him a

prisoner of the State. His papers were seized, and he was hurried before the Privy Council. The investigation lasted three quarters of an hour, and at its conclusion, he was ordered to be conveyed to the Tower in his own coach. Notwithstanding the respect with which he had been personally treated, when under his examination before the Privy Council, the usage which he afterwards experienced, when a prisoner in the Tower, was, to say the least, disgraceful to the ministry who authorised such cowardly oppression. Bishop Atterbury made a speech in his own defence before the House of Lords which lasted two hours. He was declared guilty of high treason, deprived of his benefices, and sentenced to banishment for life. On the 18th of June, 1723, Atterbury bade farewell for ever to his country. He proceeded to Paris, and there on the 15th of February, 1731, he died. His body was brought to England and buried in Westminster Abbey, on the 12th of May in the same year.

We append a reprint of a curious old broadside preserved in the British Museum relating to Atterbury's confinement in the Tower of London.

THE

Bishop of Rochester's Case ;

OR an HYMN to the

TOWER.

H ail mighty Fabrick! *England's* Magazine,
    The Ancient *Store-House* of our Kings and Queens!
Who doth within thy Stately Walls contain,
    More than my Pen can in this Room explain ;
Therefore I'll treat of Ages past and gone,
And proper Things in Silence lately done ;
And tell of Actions in Proceeding Times,
For those shall be the Subject of my Rhimes.

The Wise and Great ELIZABETH was here
Confined within thy Walls a Prisoner:
The Royal Dame, tho' born in highest State,
Cou'd not withstand the Secret Hand of Fate.
RELIGION was the Crime that brought her thither,
And thus RELIGION brings Men GOD knows whither:
Sometimes our Friends, as well as Mortal Foes,
Within thy Bounds thy circling Walls inclose,
Seven Sacred Pillars of our Church, nay, more,
The Famous LAUD, and Others long before,
For Crimes (I have not Room here to relate)
In those *Sad Times*, were Forc'd within thy Gate.
By their Confinement, whether Right or Wrong,
I need not make the subject of my SONG;
For 'tis well known, in this our Present Age,
Why these brave Men were brought upon the Stage;
Some lost their Lives in coming out from Thee,
And Others, better Fate did set them Free.
Unhappy MONMOUTH from thy Gates was led,
And on thy Towering Hill resign'd his HEAD;
But Cruel *Jefferies* died in his Bed.
Renowned FENWICK did himself Resign
Into thy Tower, which did him there Confine.
Until a Law did of him Treason Tax,
And consequently brought the Fatal AX.
There's Others since of very High Degree
Were forc'd to Make a Visit unto Thee;
Whose cross-grain'd Fate the Powers did Offend,
And brought their Lives unto a Fatal end.
But one thing more I'd almost quite forgot,
And that was Dr. *Oates's Popish Plot*;
Who strove with all his Learned Might and Main,
To send thee Crouds of Guests to entertain;
But hope such Times will never come again.

London Printed and Re-Printed in *Dublin* by *John Harding* in *Molesworth's-Court* in *Fishamble-Street*.

The following is a list of the Bishops of Rochester after Atterbury's banishment, and the dates of their appointment to the see. They probably lived more or less at Bromley Palace.

>Samuel Bradford, 1723.
>Joseph Wilcocks, 1731.
>Zachariah Pearce, 1756.
>John Thomas, 1774.
>Samuel Horsley, 1793.
>Thomas Dampier, 1802.
>Walker King, 1808.
>Hon. Hugh Percy, 1827.
>George Murray, 1827.

Bromley Palace was sold to Coles Child, Esq., in 1845, during the time of Bishop Murray.

St Blaze's Well.

Hasted, in his "History of Kent," writes—

"There is a *well* in the Bishop's grounds, near his garden here, called St Blaze's Well, which, having great resort to it antiently, on account of its medicinal virtues, had an oratory annexed to it, dedicated to that saint. It was particularly frequented at Whitsuntide, on account of a remission of forty days injoined penance, to such as should visit this chapel, and offer up their orisons in it, on the three holy days of Pentecost.

"This oratory falling to ruin at the Reformation, the well too came to be disused, and the scite of both, in process of time, became totally forgotten and unknown, and continued so till the well was again discovered in 1754."

This was published by Hasted in 1795. In the year 1756 an

interesting account of a mineral spring found at Bromley was published by Thomas Reynolds, entitled,

> "Some
> Experiments
> on the
> Chalybeat Water
> Lately discovered, near the Palace of the
> Lord Bishop of Rochester, at
> Bromley, in Kent,
> &c., &c.
> By Thomas Reynolds, Surgeon.
> "With such [Water] doth He heal Men, and taketh away their Pain."
> —Eccles. xxxviii. 7.
> London.
> M.DCC. LVI." [8⁰ pp. 69.]

This pamphlet is now of great rarity. No copy exists in the British Museum Library, although, from the nature of its matter, one would expect to find it there. A copy exists in the Library of the London Institution, at Finsbury Circus, from which we here give a few extracts :—

"The Chalybeat Water, on which the following experiments were made, arises at the foot of a declivity, a very small distance eastward from the palace of the Lord Bishop of Rochester, at Bromley in Kent. The soil through which it passes is gravel; and it issues immediately from a bed of pure white sand. The course of the spring seems to be about north-north-east and south-south-west: its opening is towards the south-south-west; and as Shooter's Hill bears about north-north-east from its aperture, it probably comes from thence. It was discovered in September MDCCLIV. by the reverend Mr Harwood, his Lordship's domestic chaplain, by means of a yellow ochrey sediment, remaining in the tract of a small current, leading from the spring to the corner of the moat, with the waters of which it used to mix.

"It is very probable that this spring has been formerly frequented; for in digging about it, there were found the remains of steps leading down to it made of oak plank, which appeared as if they had laid under ground a great many years.

"When his Lordship was acquainted that the water of this Spring had been examined, and found to be a good Chalybeat, he, with great humanity, immediately ordered it to be secured from the mixture of other waters, by skilful workmen, and enclosed in a circular brick-work like the top of a well; in hopes, that it might prove beneficial as a medicine, to such as should think fit to drink it.

"This order was speedily and effectually executed and the Water not only secured but the access to it made very commodious to the Public, by the generous care, and under the inspection of Mr Wilcox, his Lordship's son. And their benevolent intentions have already been answered with success: for great numbers of people, of all conditions, but chiefly of the middling and poorer sort, drink daily of this excellent water, many of whom have been remarkably releived from various infirmities and diseases, which were not only afflicting but dangerous."

The main object of the pamphlet is, as its title-page sets forth, to give an account of various experiments which Mr Reynolds conducted with a view of testing the medicinal virtues of the water. He shows "that the water of this spring is much richer in mineral contents than the water of Tunbridge Wells" (p. 17.) The book was reviewed very favourably in the *Gentleman's Magazine* for

April 1756, wherein are given fuller particulars of the experiments than it may be necessary to reproduce here.

Hone's "Table Book," Vol. II. pp, 65-8, contains an account of the "Bishop's Well, Bromley, Kent," which gives a few facts unmentioned by Reynolds and Hasted. Speaking of the spring, he says, "It rises so slowly, as to yield scarcely a gallon in a quarter of an hour, and is retained in a small well about sixteen inches in diameter. To the stone work of this little well a wooden cover is attached by a chain. When the fluid attains a certain height, its surplus trickles through an orifice at the side to increase the water of a moat, or small lake, which borders the grounds of the palace, and is overhung on each side with the branches of luxuriant shrubs and trees. Above the well there is a roof of thatch, supported by six pillars, in the manner of a rustic temple, heightening the picturesque appearance of the scene, so as to justify its representation by the pencil. On visiting it, with Mr W[illiams], this pleasant seclusion, consecrated by former episcopal care, and the fond recollection of ancient adjacent residents, was passing to ruin: we disturbed some boys in their work of pulling reeds from the thatched roof. A recent vacancy of the see seemed to have extended to the superintendence of the well; the seeds of neglect had germinated, and were springing up. I have revisited the spot, and seen

———————the wild briar,
'The thorn, and the thistle, grown broader and higher."

We have the pleasure of presenting our readers with a reduced fac-simile of the engraving which accompanies the foregoing account in the "Table Book."

Coles Child, Esq., the lord of the manor, and possessor of St. Blaze's Well, in a letter addressed to the present writer in 1887, said, "The well is still in existence, although the whole building, as restored by my father, was knocked into the moat during the last heavy snowstorm."

Simpson's Place.

Simpson's Place or Simpson's Manor, was an estate of great antiquity. "*Simpsons,*" says Philipot, "is the second Seat of Account, though in Ages of a later Inscription it contracted that Name, yet anciently it was the Demeasne of *Bankewell*, a Family of Signall Repute in this Track, *John de Bankewell* held a Charter of Free Warren to his Lands in *Bromley*, in which this was involved in the thirty first of *Edward* the first, and *Thomas de Bankewell* dyed feifed of it in the thirty fifth year of *Edward* the third, and when this Family was shrunk at this Place into a finall extinction; the next who were eminent in the Possession of it, were the *Clarks*, and one *William Clark* that flourished here in the Reign of *Henry* the fifth, that he might not be obnoxious to the Statute of Kernellation, obtained Licence to erect a strong little Pile of Lime and Stone, with an embattell'd Wall encircled with a deep Moat, which is supplyed and nourished with a living Spring; but this mans posterity did not long enjoy it, for about the latter end of *Henry* the sixth, *John Simpson* dwelt here by right of Purchase, and he having much improved the ancient Fabrick, setled his Name upon it, and indeed that is all that's left to Evidence they were once Owners of it, for in an Age or two after this, it was conveyed to Mr. *John Stiles* of *Beckenham* Esquire, from whom descends Sir *Humphrey Stiles* Knight and Baronet, Cupbearer to the late K. *Charles*, and him does Simpsons confesse for its instant Owner." *Philipot's* "*Villare Cantianum*," 1659, p. 84.

Philipot's account was written in 1659. Hasted's account, published in 1797, contains fuller information.

"In the 11th year of King Edward IV., Robert Simpson died possessed of this seat; his descendant, Nicholas Sympson, the king's barber, alienated Sympsons to Alexander Basset, who in the reign of Henry VIII. conveyed it by sale to Sir Humphrey Style, of Langley, son of John Style, alderman of London; this estate being then held in *socage*.

"His descendant, Humphrey Style of Langley, esq. dying without male issue, his only daughter and heir, Elizabeth, carried this estate in marriage to Sir John Elwill, bart, who dying in 1727, without issue, Edmund, his brother, succeeded him, and about 1732, conveyed Sympsons to Hugh Raymond of Great Saling, in Essex, esq., who settled it on his only son, Jones Raymond, esq., in tail general, with remainder to his eldest daughter Amy, married to Peter Burrell, esq., and her issue male. On the death of James Raymond, esq., son of Jones Raymond, before-mentioned, in 1678, without issue, Peter Burrell, of Beckenham, esq., in right of his wife became intitled to it; after the death of whose widow it descended to her grandson, Sir Peter Burrell, knt. and bart. since created lord Gwydir, and he is the present owner of it." *Hasted's Hist. of Kent.*

A lease of the estate was granted to Samuel Rickets, Esq., who sold it to Colonel Jackson, about the year 1803. The estate was sold with other estates, by Lord Gwydir, in 1830, to Robert Veitch, Esq., whose gardener occupied the house. It had been the farm residence of Jeremiah Ringer for fifty years.

In 1858 Simpson's Place was the property of Colonel Tweedy, of Bromley House.

Mr. John Dunkin made a careful examination of Simpson's Place, and the following is his account of the building, "It appears that the deep moat extended close to the walls of the ancient castellated building on the north, east, and south sides, and that the angles were secured by a strong buttress projecting into the moat. The whole extent of the foundation of the eastern wall, together with the two buttresses which still remained perfect, were found by admeasurement about 34 yards in length; and the breadth of the building, as far as could be conjectured from its ivy mantled walls on the south, about 14 or 15 yards. These foundations are built of large flints intermixed with stone and cemented with strong lime mortar. It is probable that the building was square, and entered by a drawbridge on the northern side; and from the circumstance of the wall not extending to the verge of the moat, had a small terrace on the east. The apartments inhabited by the lord of the domain probably either lined the outer wall, and were lighted from a small court in the centre, or consisted of an isolated building within the walls, as was generally the case in castellated mansions, and perhaps the best plan that could be adopted for the purpose of defence.

"The present building (1815) is formed of brick and timber, and appears to have been erected in more settled times, on a part of the foundation of the ancient structure; probably on its decay, and about the sixteenth century. The interior indicates it as designed for the residence of a gentleman of that period. The fire-place of the hall, doorways, &c. still remain, though much disfigured by the alterations occasioned by its conversion into a farm house, in which state it has remained for many years. The moat on the western and northern sides have been filled up by the present inhabitant, Mr Jeremiah Ringer, who has occupied the house for more than fifty years.

"The ancient road leading to this mansion lay through a part of what is now Col. Jackson's pleasure ground."

Mr Dunkin appends the following foot-note:—

"This time-stricken mansion offers a favourable opportunity for any daring ghost to play his vagaries; and it does not seem to have been neglected, for I was solemnly assured that noises had been often heard in and about the house, sometimes as if the furniture fell down and broke to pieces; and that once a lady appeared dressed in white, with a lighted torch in her hand, accompanied by a gentleman in dark clothes, with a high-crowned broad-brimmed hat which flapped over the sides of his face!!! ... After this marvellous occurrence I presume my reader is prepared to hear any other wonder; and therefore I take the opportunity of informing him there is a tradition that Bromley church was first attempted to be built at Wigmore, but what the workmen built by day was carried away by night, and fixed on the spot where it now stands, so that the architect was at last obliged to acquiesce, and then the building regularly proceeded!!!"—*Dunkin's "Outlines of the History and Antiquities of Bromley,"* 1815.

Simpson's Place is now swept away, and its site is occupied by modern buildings. It has been said that Henry VIII. and Charles II. both paid visits to this place, but there does not appear to be much ground for the tradition.

One drawing of Simpson's Place, in black and white, the date of which is probably about the year 1800, is preserved in the Library of George III. at the British Museum. The accompanying illustration is a reduced tracing of that drawing.

SIMPSON'S PLACE, BROMLEY, KENT.
(*From a Drawing in the King's Library, British Museum.*)

The estate of Simpson's comprised only a moderate amount of land in Bromley, but those who possessed this place originally held a large tract in the parishes of Beckenham, West Wickham, and Hayes. Indeed this last-mentioned portion of the Simpson's property must have comprised a great portion of the land included in the Saxon charter of 862, which was not afterwards conferred upon the church.

THE MANOR OF SUNDRIDGE.

This manor was the next in importance to that held by the Bishop of Rochester. To the latter Sundridge appears to have been subservient, as, although its owners enjoyed manorial rights, they originally held it under the Bishop. The family of Blund, or Blound, who were anciently lords of Guisnes in France, formerly resided here. One of them had three sons, who came into England with William the Conqueror. Of these, one returned to France, and the other two, Sir Robert and Sir William, remained in England, the former settling in Suffolk, and the latter in Lincolnshire. From these individuals the several families of Blount in this kingdom have descended. Of a younger branch of them was Peter le Blund, who owned Sundridge in the reign of Henry III., in the 39th year of which he was made Constable of the Tower of London. His descendant, Edward de Blund, was possessed of Sundridge in the 20th year of King Edward III. Soon after, this family ended in a female heir, who carried this seat in marriage to Willoughby; from which name some years after it passed by purchase to Booth, whose descendant, William Booth, died possessed of the manor of Sundridge, held of the Bishop of Rochester by knight service, and by the service of making suit at the court of the palace. Robert Booth, his son and heir, was, with one hundred other gentlemen of this county, made Knight of the Bath in the 17th year of that reign. Sundridge continued in the possession of his descendants, until Sith Booth, Esq., dying without male issue, one of his daughters and co-heirs carried it in marriage to Thomas Bettenham, of Shurland, in Pluckley, Esq., whose great-grandson, Stephen Bettenham, of Bromley, gentleman, gave it in marriage with his daughter Anne, to Robert Pynsent, third son of John Pynsent, of Chudleigh, in Devonshire. He died here in 1679, without issue, and was buried in the chancel of Bromley Church. He was succeeded in the possession of this seat and estate by Thomas Washer, of Lincoln's Inn, Esq., on whose death, in 1720, it came to his son, John Washer, Esq., who died without male issue in 1749. His only daughter and heir carried Sundridge in marriage to William Wilson, Esq., Sheriff of this county in 1766. He died possessed of it in 1776, and his eldest son alienated it to Edward George Lind. Esq. In 1796 Sundridge was purchased by Sir Claud Scott, Bart., who pulled down the old house and built the present handsome mansion for his own residence. It has since remained in the possession of the Scott family.

The situation of Sundridge Park is very beautiful, and the surrounding richly wooded hills afford some very fine views. The mansion stands on a hill which was considerably lowered when the house was erected, in order to give it an appropriate elevation and suitable aspect. The three celebrated architects, Messrs Repton, Nash, and Wyatt have each bestowed a share of their skill upon this charming residence. The principal front is adorned with three porticos, one in the centre and one at each end. That in the centre is circular, supported by six columns, and surmounted by a dome; the other two have each four columns, supporting a pediment. They are all of the Corinthian order. A good engraving of Sundridge Park, published Jan. 1, 1820, may be found in Neale's "*Views of the Seats of Noblemen and Gentlemen,*" 2nd Series, Vol. V. From Hasted's account it would appear that Sundridge acquired the name of Washer's in the Woods, doubtless from the family of Washer, who were formerly possessed of the place, and that it was known by that name at the end of the last century.

BLACKBROOK.

Blackbrok, or Blackbrook, was an estate separated from the chief manor at an early date. There is reason to think that this estate was, as we have before stated, situated at or near Southborough. There is a Blackbrook Farm about a mile from Bickley Railway Station. Dr Beeby's paper on the "Church and Manor of Bromley" contains the following particulars of the estate:—

"Blackbrook was held by Sir Thomas Latymer, to whose father a charter of free warren was granted in 1329, and the Latymers conveyed the estate to Richard Lacer and Juliana his wife. In the Close Roll, 7th year of Edward III., are two deeds recording the transfer of Blackbrok and other lands in Bromley to Richard Lacer, who also possessed property in Deptford. He was Mayor of London, and assisted in punishing the abettors of the rebellion under the Earl of Kent. Lacer married a second time, and there is a memorial brass in Bromley Church to his wife Isabella, who died 1361.

"As applied to a spot near Blackbrook, we find marked on old maps and inserted in ancient charters the names of South-barrow and South-borough. For many years a residence has been so indicated, which formerly was inhabited by a certain Andrew Beadle, one of whose family is mentioned in the 43rd year of Elizabeth. It has from time to time received various additions.

"At a short distance is a place of considerable antiquity, called Turpington Farm, which tradition points out as the site of the court house of the first lords of Blackbrook. Writing in 1797, Wilson in his history of Bromley says 'I heard this place was famous for having been an ancient barony of one of the feudal lords; was shewn a farm-house that had been the barons' court-house; another which had been the jail.'"

Mr Robinson Latter, of Pixfield, has in his possession an original deed being a conveyance from Sir Edmund Style to Richard Thornhill in the 19th of Elizabeth of a property comprising about thirteen acres of land. Dr Beeby identifies this property with the whole east side of the High Street, from the Bell Inn up to and including the grounds now occupied by Bromley College. In 1532 one Thomas Knight owned this property, as also Tuppingdens, near Blackbrook, and ninety-four acres of land at Bromley Common, called Goodwyns, which Dr Beeby connects with Cooper's Farm.

"Thomas Knight is described as a citizen of London, and 'Pandoxator,' *i.e.*, a brewer and seller of his own beer. He had a son Robert, who contributed twenty marks to the loan to Henry VIII., 1542; and the next owner, John Knight, probably sold the estate to Style, who conveyed it to one Richard Thornhill, who settled it on his son Samuel, who died during his father's lifetime, and thus the property came back to Richard Thornhill. This

Richard married twice, his second wife being a daughter of William Watson of Frindsbury. He died in the year 1600, and there is a large brass to the memory of himself and wives in Bromley Church. Subsequently the house and grounds were held by John Thornhill, in the 4th of Charles I.

"It may not be uninteresting to mention that Dr Hawkesworth, editor of the 'Adventurer,' lived afterwards in this mansion, which belonged to the Knights and Thornhills.

"There are in the possession of Mr Latter about twenty-three panels of very deeply and elegantly cut oak carving, in the best style of the Tudor period; on which both the name and initials of Thomas Knight occur in several instances. Their date is identified with the period in which the above-named Thomas Knight lived, by the occurrence, on several of the panels, of the well known badges of Catherine of Arragon and Henry VIII., as the castle of Castile, the sheaf of arrows, the pomegranate slipped, the portcullis and Tudor rose. One also bears the royal coat of arms of Henry VII., used also for a time by Henry VIII., the supporters being a dragon dexter, and the greyhound collared sinister. Two of the panels also bear the arms and shields of William Warham, Archbishop of Canterbury, 1504 to 1532. There are also several ecclesiastical emblems, such as the five wounds encircled by a crown of thorns, the monogram I.H.S.; also an emblematical device representing sin as a bird with a dagger, attacking an angel who bears a shield, and numerous figures of angels and cherubs; from which it has been inferred that probably the panels formed a portion of the rood screen of Bromley Church. They were found by their present owner about thirty years since, covered with numerous coats of paint, the greater part of which has been removed with infinite labour and trouble, owing to the thickness and number of the coats of various colour, in some parts fully half an inch deep, and nearly obliterating the carving. They then lined a cupboard in a house in the town of Bromley, which was built about 1796, upon part of the land formerly belonging to the mansion owned by Thomas Knight, which had then recently been purchased and pulled down by the builder of the house in which they were found. This may be taken to make it probable that they formed part of the materials of the old mansion; but it so happens that the same builder, in the year 1792, as appears by the parish register, accepted a contract for £1300, to renew and make alterations in the church, and therefore, having regard to the ecclesiastical character of the subjects of the carving, as the old materials removed from the church would become the property of the contractor, it is at least an open question whether they were not removed from that edifice, and used in the construction of his house."—*Dr Beeby.*

BROMLEY HILL PLACE.

Bromley Hill Place is on the confines of Lewisham, near Beckingham, and was the seat of the Right Hon. Sir Charles Long, afterwards Lord Farnborough.

In 1747 Captain Charles Long was rated in the Parish Books at £18. He, or an ancestor probably, went to Lewisham after the sub-division of the property of the Fitzes. Their families had been neighbours at Tavistock or Whitchurch, where the Longs had settled, perhaps in consequence of the marriage of Sir William Russell with Elizabeth Long, of Cambridgeshire, mother of Francis, fourth Earl of Bedford. She died in 1611. This information is taken from Dr. H. H. Drake's new edition of "Hasted's History of Kent, Part I., Hundred of Blackheath," p. 255. Upon page 256 of the same valuable volume there is printed a scrap pedigree of Long, from whence it appears that the pedigrees hitherto printed of Lord Farnborough's branch are in some measure erroneous.

The Right Hon. Charles Long was made a Privy Councillor of England and Ireland on Jan. 13th 1802, a Lord Commissioner of the Treasury, May, 1804; Secretary of State for Ireland, 1806; Paymaster General, April, 1807, and again in 1813; and he was created Baron Farnborough, of Bromley Hill Place, August 1826. He was a Commissioner of the Land Tax, Chairman of the Committee for the Inspection of National Monuments, a Commissioner for the Duchy of Cornwall, a Trustee of the British and Hunterian Museums, and of the National Gallery, Deputy President of the British Institution, F.R.S., and F.S.A.

He was the third son of Beeston Long, Esq., of Carshalton, a very eminent West India merchant, by Susannah, daughter and heiress of Abraham Crop, Esq., of Richmond. He was entered at Emanuel College, Cambridge, about the year 1778.

In January, 1789, he first entered Parliament as one of the members for Rye, and in 1791 he was appointed Joint Secretary to the Treasury. He was re-elected for the same borough in the next year. In 1796 he was returned for Midhurst, and in 1802 for Wendover. As an intelligent man of office and a ready speaker, he made himself very useful to Mr. Pitt, with whom he retired in July 1801, and on whose return to power in 1804 he was made a Lord Commissioner of the Treasury, as before said. He was re-elected for Haslemere at the general elections of 1812, 1818, and 1820. He was a staunch partizan and Tory; but he seldom or never spoke in the House, except on matters of business connected with his official situation.

He was held in much esteem by George III., and with his successor he was in habits of more familiar intercourse; and was consulted by him on all subjects connected with the improvement of the royal palaces. At Bromley Hill Place he entertained George IV., William IV., and Queen Adelaide.

His beautiful domain at Bromley Hill, the creation of himself and his accomplished lady, was purchased by him in 179--, having then nothing to distinguish it from the ordinary class of suburban villas. It possessed however the advantage of being in the close vicinity to the favourite retreat of Mr. Pitt, Holwood Hill, in the parish of Keston; and for nearly forty years he found a delightful recreation in adorning and heightening its natural beauties.

Lord Farnborough was a person of considerable taste and accomplishment, particularly in paintings. Sir Benjamin Hobhouse, in some debate, called him "the Vitruvius of the present age." He printed a pamphlet, we believe, for private circulation, on the projected improvements and alterations then proposed to be carried into effect in the metropolis. The title is "Remarks on the Improvements of London," 1826, 8°. He was also the author of a sketch of the character of Pitt, which he wrote for Gifford's life of that great statesman.

Lord Farnborough died at his seat, Bromley Hill Place, January 17th, 1838, and was interred on the 27th of January at Wormley in Hertfordshire. His property was chiefly divided among his three nephews, Colonel Long of the Guards, who succeeded to Bromley Hill Place, the Rev. Charles Maitland Long, and William Long, Esq., of Hurt's Hill.

In the year 1811 George Cumberland published a sketch of "Bromley Hill, the seat of the Right Hon. Charles Long, M.P." From this tract we give some extracts.

"All that there was here to work on was a fine rising knoll, a few acres of wood on a little hill, three or four low meadows, a winding brook that skirted them, and a small head of pure water; but the surrounding scenery was well wooded, well varied with interesting objects, and the skirts of the horizon what I may be allowed to call, well fringed, and well degraded. How that knoll, that wood, and those meadows have been treated, and with what masterly taste they have been transformed, must now be the subject of my eulogium.

"There are two entrances from the high road; one by a common park gate on the top of the hill which conducts to a private way that crosses the estate by the Mansion; the other, its proper entrance from the Metropolis, of the most unassuming form; a real cottage lodge, with few ornaments to distinguish it from other habitations of the sort, and which perhaps *ought to be* a little more dressed. This entrance conducts by a gently rising road, where gravel is dug on the spot, through a lawn judiciously broken, into groups of trees that conceal the boundary up to the house, which crowns very handsomely the summit of the hill. It is a modern villa, of a compact form, well broken into masses by varied angles.

"The entrance, which has no porch, opens into a covered and glazed corridor of some length, ornamented with bronzes, busts, candelabra, and large China vases; and leads to a handsome flight of steps that delivers the guests to a hall, from whence are the passages to a dining room, breakfasting room, anti-room, and library, drawing room, that opens into a very handsome conservatory dressed with trellisses.

"This agreeable library is ornamented with some large pieces of rare China on brackets and slabs, and gives an entrance, through the conservatory, to a singular flower garden that has the best feature of the old taste preserved; the inclosed terrace with its sun dial, low wall for flower pots, vases, &c., and shaded at both ends by two or three well grown pinasters; its position also is very favourable, as the sun rises behind it, and its pensile garden, covered with rock plants, cheddar pinks, &c., crawling over large masses of the aggregate fossils found in the neighbourhood which contains rounded pebbles, oyster shells, scallops, and many others. From this little antique terrace the view commands, at times, St Paul's Church, its dome and turret towers appearing as if banded with white, and beyond extend the Highgate and Hampstead Hills, forming a broad line of back ground; but that which renders the scene still more remarkably interesting is, that you see nothing of London except its spires, and the great church seems to arise like a vision from the edges of a wooded hill. Shooter's Hill, Blackheath, and, best of all, Sydenham Common, makes a noble distance, owing to its long lines and purple tints of heath. The pictures within the house are not many, but they are well chosen; a *Reynolds*, a *Gainsborough*, a *Mola*, a *Teniers*, a *Poussin*, and, above all, a landscape by *Reubens* that cannot be matched for excellence, and although not one of his largest, is certainly one of his *very best*. Also a large picture by Canaletti of a canal in Venice, now in the National Gallery, the famous "White Horse," by Vandyck, and the infant, "Samuel," by Joshua Reynolds. In the drawing room there is, or was, one of the last marble busts that Canova ever executed, and a beautiful statue of Flora, by Westmacott, in the entrance hall. One only thing we have to regret—that we can there find none of Mrs Long's incomparable views, who certainly is admitted to be equal to any artist of the present day, and whose landscapes exhibited annually at the Royal Academy have never been rivalled, even when put into competition with practical professors, and placed side by side with their happiest efforts."

The little book has a good deal more information in reference to the water scenery, the wood, and the pleasure grounds; but it is hardly of a sufficiently definite character for our purpose.

Another edition of the book, containing additional matter, was printed in 1816.

BROMLEY COLLEGE.

Dr. John Warner, Bishop of Rochester, by his Will, bearing date 4th of September, 1666, only five weeks before his death, bequeathed the sum of £8,500 for the construction of a Hospital or College for the reception of "Twenty poore widowes" and a Chaplain. The executors of this Will were the Lord Chief Justice Bridgman, Sir Philip Warwick, Knt., Dr. Thomas Peirce, President of Magdalen College, Oxford, and Dr. John Lee, Archdeacon of Rochester. To accomplish this generous object, he directed his executors to raise, out of his personal estate, a building proper for this purpose, and he charged his manor of Swayton in Lincolnshire, with the annual payment of £450. Of this sum he directed that each widow should receive £20 per annum, and the Chaplain £50 per annum. The stipulation was made that the Chaplain should always be chosen from Magdalene College, Oxford, of which College Warner himself had been a fellow. The founder had expressed a desire that the building should be erected as near to Rochester as conveniently might be, but as no healthy or convenient spot could be found near that place, power was given by an Act of Parliament, passed in 1670 (for the purpose of explaining and settling some parts of the Bishop's donation), to build it anywhere within the diocese, according to the discretion of the executors, who fixed on the present site at the north end of the town of Bromley. The founder not having made any provision for repairs, his executors, with the consent of the heir-at-law, charged the said manor of Swayton with the further sum of £5 per annum; but this being thought insufficient, the executors generously gave one hundred pounds each, with which a fee-farm rent of £10 was purchased; but still this sum was found to be much too small to keep the fabric in decent repair, and the trustees have been at times under the necessity of soliciting voluntary contributions for that purpose.

The building of Bromley College probably was commenced in or soon after the year 1670. It has been said that some of the bricks of which it is built, were brought from the debris of the great fire of London in 1666.

By an inquisition, taken under a Commission of Charitable Uses, 28th March, 1693, reciting the Will of Bishop Warner, and the Act of Parliament, it was found that a Hospital was, within a few years after the said Act, built near the town of Bromley, called Bromley College,[1] that twenty clergymen's widows had been placed therein, according to the direction of the Founder's Will, and the

---

[1] This appears to be the first instance in which the place was called Bromley College. Previous to that date it was known as Bishop Warner's Hospital.

vacancies, as they had occurred, had been supplied; that £20 had been customarily paid to them at the four usual feasts till within the last six or seven years; but that several of the said widows were then in arrear, which arrears ought to be paid by Lee Warner, Esq. The Commissioners, by their decree of the same date, being satisfied that the non-payments of the said Charity and other miscarriages had happened in great measure owing to there not being any Trustees duly appointed for inspecting and governing the said Charity; but that the same had been lately managed by the said Lee Warner, the owner of the manor, charged with the sum of £455, ordered that the Archbishop of Canterbury, the Bishop of London, the Bishop of Rochester, the Judge of the Prerogative Court of Canterbury, the Chancellor to the Bishop of Rochester, the Dean of St Paul's, and the Archdeacon of Rochester for the time respectively, and Sir Stephen Lennard, Sir John Shawe, and Sir John Morden, Barts.; Abraham Harrison and Philip Boddenham, Esqs., should be Trustees for the said Charity; and that they should have full power to make such orders and rules for the well government of the said College and the due execution of the trust as to them should seem meet and convenient; that they should receive the said sum of £455 from the owners of the manor of Swayton, and should dispose and distribute the same amongst the said widows and Chaplain, and in the repairs of the College from time to time, according to the directions of the said Will and Act of Parliament, and that it should be lawful for the survivors and successors of the official Trustees to elect one or more worthy persons in the place of any non-official Trustee deceased, to make up the number of twelve, as in their discretion should be thought meet. It was further ordered that the Trustees for the time being should, within forty days after the vacancy of the place of any of the widows, or of the Chaplain, elect another widow or Chaplain, duly qualified, according to the Will and Act of Parliament.

In the year 1735 a two-leaved folio tract was printed, entitled, "The State of Bromley College, in Kent." After giving a statement of the foundation and history of the charity, the writer of the tract says :—

"But tho' this power be given by *Parliament*, yet no addition has hitherto been made to this *Charitable Foundation*, excepting what is already mentioned. Nor have any *Legacies* been left towards the support of the Fabrick, besides two, one by Mr Archdeacon *Plume*, and the other by Archbishop Tenison; which have been long ago expended upon it. The *Trustees* themselves have likewise made voluntary contributions for its Repairs; but the building, thro' a gradual Decay, is still in a bad state, and will require every year a much greater Sum to keep it in a substantial and decent Condition than what the Fund now settled can possibly supply; and consequently it must go entirely to ruin without further Assistance. For which Reasons it is thought proper to publish this short Account of it, that Persons who have Hearts and Abilities to do charitable Works of this kind, may be put in mind of a very fit and real Object.

"The Object indeed seems so fit that one cannot but think, had it been more known, it would before this time have been better provided for, if by no other persons, yet by *Incumbents* within the *Diocese* of *Rochester*, including the *Deanery* of *Shoreham*, which is within the *peculiar* Jurisdiction of the *Archbishop* of *Canterbury*, because the *Widows* of such *Incumbents*, if in want of such a Charity, are always to have the Preference in every Election. However, as this *Charity* has extended itself very often into other *Dioceses*, it may be hoped, that Benefactions to it may be equally extensive, especially if it be consider'd, that should the *Fund* grow prosperous, the Buildings of the *College* might not only be repair'd but enlarged; nay, Provision might be made for the future Maintenance of a greater number of *Widows*, who might be chosen out of any other *Dioceses*, if *Benefactions* should come from thence; and the *Benefactors* and *Trustees* should agree therein, as they have full Power to do by the Act of Parliament,

"But that all *Benefactors* may be satisfied, what likelihood there is of a faithful and wise disposal or management of their *Charity*, it must be proper to let them know who are the *Trustees of Bromley College*. They are *Twelve* in Number, *seven* by verture of their Stations or Offices, and *five* by Election, whose Names follow:—

By *Station* or *Office*.

William Lord Archbishop of *Canterbury*,
Edmund Lord Bishop of *London*,
Joseph Lord Bishop of *Rochester*,
Francis Lord Bishop of *Chichester*, as Dean of *St Paul's*, London.
Dr *John Bettesworth*, Judge of the Prerogative Court of *Canterbury*.
Dr *Humphrey Henchman*, Chancellor of the *Diocese* of *Rochester*,
Dr *John Denne*, Archd. of *Rochester*.

By Election.

Lee Warner, Esq., of *Walsingham*, in *Norfolk*;
William Tryon, Esq., of *Chislehurst*, in *Kent*;
William Morris, Esq., of *Kensington*;
Peter Burrell, Esq., of *Beckenham*, in *Kent*;
William Emmett, Esq., of *Bromley*, in *Kent*;

Rev. Daniel Lysons, in his "Environs of London," published in 1811, mentions that the following is a list of the Trustees of Bromley College at that time:—

>The Archbishop of Canterbury,
>The Bishop of London,
>The Bishop of Rochester,
>The Archdeacon of Rochester,
>The Chancellor of Rochester,
>The Dean of St Paul's,
>The Dean of Arches,
>The Right Hon. Lord Viscount Sydney,
>Sir Vicary Gibbs, the Attorney-General,
>Sir Beaumont Hotham,
>George Lee Warner, Esq.,
>Multon Lambard, Esq.,
>George Norman, Esq., Treasurer.

Bromley College was exempted from the payment of taxes by an Act of Parliament passed in 1757.

Among the papers and documents relating to the College in the custody of the Chaplain is the Treasurer's Book, in which is contained an account of the payments of allowances to the widows. The entries in the book date from the year 1791, and are of special value as showing who have been the inmates of the College since that date. Each lady formerly signed her name in the Treasurer's Book upon the receipt of her money. The Treasurer's accounts are quite complete from the year 1791 up to the present time. From a hasty glance through the book, I find that Peter Burrell, Esq., was Treasurer in the year 1768, and that in the year

1776 James Norman, Esq., was Treasurer. A member of the family of Norman has been Treasurer of the College ever since that date, and up to the present time.

Bromley College consists of two quadrangles, with colonnades in the interior. The principal entrance is a handsome piece of work executed in Bath stone. At the top are the arms of Bishop Warner, *quarterly 1st and 4th per pale indented ar. and sa.; 2nd and 3rd az. a fleur-de-lis or*, impaled with the arms of the See of Rochester. Immediately underneath is the following inscription:—

> DEO ET ECCLESIÆ.
> THIS COLLEGE FOR TWENTY POORE
> WIDOWES (OF ORTHODOX & LOYALL
> CLERGYMEN) & A CHAPLIN WAS
> GIVEN BY IOHN WARNER LATE LD.
> BISHOP OF ROCHESTER,
> 1666.

The whole of the west front is part of the original college. There are from this front two projecting wings, being the residences for the chaplain and the treasurer. Upon entering the college by the chief entrance the first grass-covered quadrangle is seen. This first quadrangle and the chaplain's and treasurer's houses were the original building of Bp. Warner's executors. It is a spot of great beauty and seclusion. The entrance to the college chapel is at the east end of the quadrangle. The original chapel occupied much the same position as the present building, but it differed greatly from it in its architectural proportions. Its roof was flat, and it was built much in the same form as the rooms of the college. Amongst its interior ornamental features were portraits in oil colours of Bishop Warner and Bishop Pearce, both of which paintings are now preserved in the chaplain's apartments. The old chapel was built in the spurious Italian style, introduced into England in the reign of Charles II., having round-headed windows, intersected by a single stone mullion, and heavy portcullis iron bars; a high cornice, surmounted by a flat lath and plaster ceiling, and walls lined half-way up with panelling; forming together with the Italian colonnades an incongruous mixture with the late Jacobean of the remainder of the quadrangle. It was insufficient for the requirements of the inmates, who had increased in the proportion of nearly seven to one since the foundation of the college. The new chapel, erected from the designs of Messrs Waring and Blake, is built in the early decorated style.

The second quadrangle of the New College is east of the Old College and Chapel. Of this quadrangle ten of the tenements were built with the legacy of Mrs Bettinson, and completed in 1794, and the other ten with the legacy of Mr William Pearce, and completed in 1805. The houses of the college are forty in number, each with a separate entrance passage, comfortable sitting-room and bedroom above, a smaller bedroom over the entrance passage, and a kitchen.

The college stands upon about four acres of land, the ground not built upon being used as a garden and pleasure ground for the widows. A piece of ground, about two or three acres in size, adjoining the college, and occupying the whole length of the east wall of the college garden, was purchased by the Trustees in 1830, partly by the sale of stock and partly by subscription.

In the year 1840 Mrs Sheppard left upwards of seven thousand pounds for building and endowing five houses for the daughters of the widows who resided with their mothers in Bromley College.

These houses, now known as the Sheppard College, stand a little to the north-east of the main block. Upon one of the gables is the following inscription:—

> IN DEI GLORIAM.
> ANNO CHRISTI M DCCCXL
> HAEC DOMICILIA IN VSVM VIRGINVM
> ORBARVM QVARVM MATRES IN
> VIDVARVM COLLEGIVM VICINVM OLIM
> ADSVMPTAE FVERANT EXTRVI JVSSIT
> VIDVA THOMAE SHEPPARD, S.T.P. SOCII
> QVONDAM APVD OXON. MAGDALENENSIS
> INSVPER EASDEM ANNVIS
> PENSIONIBVS DONAVIT.

The Lodge and Entrance Gates were added to Bromley College in 1860.

The following benefactions to Bromley College are noted in the College books, and were formerly inscribed on four large tablets affixed to the walls of the Chapel, and on some of the panels beneath them:—

		£	s.	d.
1666.	Dr John Warner, Bishop of Rochester, founded it, and paid by his executors for the building	8,500	0	0
	He gave by his will, for the support of the chaplain and widows, the yearly sum of	450	0	0
	His heir gave for repairs the yearly sum of	5	0	0
	The Lord Keeper, Sir Orlando Bridgman, gave for ditto the yearly sum of	12	0	0
1704.	Dr Thomas Plume, Archdeacon of Rochester, by his will, gave for ditto,	100	0	0
1716.	Dr Thomas Tennison, Archbishop of Canterbury, by his will, gave for ditto.	52	10	0

		£	s	d
1737.	Mr Clarke, Archdeacon of Norwich, gave for ditto	5	5	0
1757.	—— Wilcocks, Esq., for building the east wall of the meadow	112	0	0
	Mrs Swift, of Bromley, by her will, gave for repairs	10	0	0
1764.	Mrs Wolfe, of Blackheath, by her will, gave for ditto	500	0	0
1767.	The Rev. Mr Alexander Jephson, Rector of Crake, in the diocese of Durham, by his will, gave for ditto	200	0	0
1768.	Dr Thomas Secker, Archbishop of Canterbury, by his will, for ditto	500	0	0
1770.	The Rev. Mr W. Hetherington, of North Cray, in his life-time, gave for the benefit of the widows, in Old South Sea Annuities	2,000	0	0
1773.	The Countess Dowager Gower, executrix to her father, the late Earl of Thanet	500	0	0
1774.	Dr Pearce, Bishop of Rochester, gave for augmenting the yearly salaries of the widows and chaplain, in Old South Sea Annuities	5,000	0	0
1782.	Mr William Pearce, brother of Bishop Pearce, left, after the decease of his great-niece (without issue), for building and endowing ten new houses	12,000	0	0
	And per annum of the interest for the chaplain	20	0	0

1784. Mrs Rogers, by will, for repairs	£120	0 0
1787. The Rev. Mr Bagshaw left in the Three per Cents., to increase the salary of the chaplain	200	0 0
1788. Mrs Helen Bettinson, by will, for building and endowing ten new houses	10,000	0 0
1793. Dr John Thomas, late Bishop of Rochester, left to be divided among the widows of the old foundation then resident	100	0 0
And to be funded and the interest applied for repairs	300	0 0
1821. Mrs Goodwin, of Haddlestone, by will	500	0 0
Miss Jane Brooke, of Norwich, for the chapel and supplying the College with water	230	0 0
1822. Mrs Carpenter, for Bible and Prayer Book	10	0 0
1823. Dr Walker King, Bishop of Rochester, gave in Three per Cent. Consols, that the interest might pay three widows (out-pensioners) £30 a year each	3,000	0 0
1824. Mrs Rose, formerly a widow of the College, by her will, to the widows of the Bromley College	8,000	0 0
1827. Magdalen College, Oxford, for the College Grove	20	0 0
1829. George Norman, Esq., late Treasurer of College for thirty-two years, gave in his life	500	0 0
1838. Right Hon. Lord Farnborough	500	0 0

1840.	Mrs Sheppard, £1250, and £6400 for building and endowing a College for the Daughters of the widows who have resided with their mothers in Bromley College	£1,250 6,400	0 0	0 0
1842.	A further gift to the same . .	2,000	0	0
1843.	Ditto, for founding out-pensions . .	2,000	0	0
1844.	£100 annually, half from the Corporation of the Sons of the Clergy, and half from the Cholmondeley Charities, for payment of the medical officers			
1854.	Collected by the Rev. J. T. B. Landon, late Chaplain, for erecting a turret and clock	126	0	0
1860.	Peter Sutton, Esq., by will . . .	100	0	0
1860.	Collected by the Rev. H. C. Adams, for building a Porter's Lodge . .	180	0	0
1861.	Mrs Green, of Southampton, by will .	100	0	0
1863.	Collected by the Rev. H. C. Adams, for rebuilding the College Chapel . .	1806	2	6

The following is a summary of the property and income of Bromley College derived from the sources above mentioned.

Rent-charges on the Manor of Swayton, Lincolnshire	£455	0	0
Fee-farm Rent out of the Borough of Southwark	10	0	0
Land at Bromley Common	1	10	0
Carry forward,	£466	10	0

Brought forward,	£466	10	0
Garden adjoining the College	30	0	0
Ground rent of Sheppard, part of said garden	6	0	0
£42,100 Consols	1263	0	0
£8148, 14s. 7d. reduced,	244	9	2
	£2009	19	2

The following are the Annual Disbursements of Bromley College:—

Forty widows, £38 a year each	£1520	0	0
Three out-pensioners, Bishop King's gift of £30 a year	90	0	0
Chaplain's Salary	150	0	0
Ditto as Secretary, for stationery and postage	5	0	0
Insurance in the Sun Fire Office	6	15	0
Servants for work of various sorts about the College	67	5	0
Gas	30	0	0
Sundries	45	0	0
	£1914	0	0

BROMLEY CHURCH.

The *Registrum Roffense* mentions a church at Bromley, but the Domesday Book is silent upon that point. Dr Beeby suggests that possibly public services were held in a chapel within the episcopal residence. It is on record that the sum of 9d., the amount due from a parish church, was paid by Bromley for chrism rent,* about forty years after the Domesday account was compiled. The existing church is the work of various dates, and has been much altered several times. If there were a church in Norman times it is difficult to trace any remains of it in the present edifice, but the font is of a distinctly Norman character. The following conspectus will show the probable dates of the building and additions to the church. It has been compiled from the best available authorities upon the subject.

A.D. 1100—1200. Norman font of carved Bethersden marble, now existing in the church.

1200—1300. Small recess on north side of the Communion Table. It was originally situated in the north wall of the chancel, and was probably an easter sepulchre.

1300—1400. During the 14th century the whole of the ancient parts of the church, including the tower, were built or rebuilt.

1764. A western gallery was built.

1773. The bells were recast.

1778. An upper western gallery was built.

1792. The north aisle was built.

1800. The pews were repaired.

1830. General renovation and rebuilding of the body of the church, and the turret was added to the tower.

---

* Chrism rent was a tribute anciently paid to the Bishop by the parish clergy for their chrism, or consecrated oil for baptism, &c. It was consecrated at Easter for the ensuing year.

1855. The lych-gate was built.
1873. Restoration of the church and tower.
1884. New chancel, south chancel aisle, and new vestry with organ chamber above were built.

"Briefly," says Dr W. T. Beeby, "the present church when built seems to have consisted of a nave with small chancel, a chantry chapel, and south aisle, the latter communicating by a large archway with the interior of an embattled tower, which had square-headed belfry windows, and was supported by diagonal buttresses."

The following is a useful summary of some of the chief points of architectural interest in Bromley church, extracted from Sir Stephen Glynne's "Notes on the Churches of Kent":—

"This church has a nave with aisles, a chancel, and a tower at the west end of the nave. The latter is Rectilinear, and built of flints, embattled, containing eight bells and a clock. The exterior of the church is much modernised. The original church consisted only of a nave and south aisle, the north aisle having been erected in 1792 at the expense of the then Bishop of Rochester. The south door is enriched with some curious wood carving, and has a singular old rude lock. In the interior the arches and piers have been removed, in order to facilitate the erection of galleries, excepting only the two west piers on the south, which are of octagonal form. The south aisle is carried to the west wall of the tower, and the west portion of it has a wood coved roof. There are north, south, and west galleries, the latter containing a fine organ. The chancel is small, but has a chapel on the south. The east window is large, and the arch supported within by shafts apparently Early Curvilinear; the mouldings of the arch are bold and good, but the tracery is gone, and most part walled up. In the north wall of the chancel is an arch of Curvilinear character, with triangular canopy, deep mouldings, feathering and shafts, with rich flowered capitols; within this arch was formerly a tomb, now destroyed. There is also a brass to one of the name of Thornhill, of about 1600, well preserved. The font is early, of square form, and a black marble, moulded with plain, semicircular arches. The pedestal is modern."

It should be explained that Sir Stephen's notes were made in 1829. Subsequent alterations of the church are nearly sufficient to account for the writer's inaccuracies. The font is of grey, Bethersden marble. It is 2 feet 4 inches square, and each of the four sides is ornamented with four semicircular-headed small panels. It has been described as being like the font in Merstham church, Surrey, and, upon examination, I find that it is of very close resemblance, the chief difference being that the Merstham font has five panels on each side, and has certain ornamental features in its upper part which are wanting in that at Bromley. They are both evidently of Norman date.

The following letter, written in 1829, appears in the *Gentleman's Magazine*, vol. xcix. pt. 2, pp. 201–2.

Sep. 13 [1829].

" Mr Urban,

" Passing through the town of Bromley, in Kent, the other day, I found the old Church there nearly pulled down, nothing remaining but the well-built Gothic tower, and portions of the side walls. The gates of the churchyard were fortified with a palisade, so that it was impossible for an antiquary to enter, and satisfy himself what might be the probable result to ancient vestiges in the Church of such desecrating and destructive appearances. I beg, therefore, through the medium of your pages, to point out to those who respect and may be able to protect the antiquities attached to Bromley Church, the matters which are peculiarly worthy their vigilance. Imprimis. There is a fine ancient font, if not of the Saxon, certainly of the earliest times of the Norman period. It is square, sufficiently large for the immersion of the infant, and the sides are ornamented with ranges of plain circular arches. Any improvement of the situation of this relic would be to remove the clumsy pedestal of brick on which it stands, and supply it with a circular supporting pillar at each angle, after the example of many fonts of the same time existing.

"There is a curious ornamental Gothic arch of the early part of the 13th century, in the north wall of the chancel. This has been conjectured (I believe erroneously) to be a tomb: it is rather the *sepulchre*, in which in Popish times the interment and resurrection of our Saviour was represented on the commencement of the festival of Easter.

"There has been a fine east window, the elegant pointed arch still remains; the arch should be re-opened and the tracery of the interweaving mullions restored from a good example. Some heraldic coats might be placed in the window with good effect. The Corinthian altar-piece, which has hitherto so glaringly violated the unity of design, should be entirely removed. The windows should be re-gothicised; about half a century since they were all deprived of their proper character. There are some brasses and memorials in the Church worthy of more particular preservation; I would not imply that it is other than a barbarous sacrilege to destroy *any* monuments of the dead. Of modern sepulchral tablets, Dr Hawkesworth's against the wall of the north aisle is remarkable for its beautiful inscription. So is Mrs Elizabeth Monk's at the exterior east end of the Church.

"The Church door is a good specimen of the taste for ornament prevailing in the 14th century; a few mouldings in oak, after the original model, nailed on in the defective places, would restore it to its original appearance.

"The *cockney cupola* should be removed from the tower, which needs little further attention, but that a fine western window in the lower stage is bricked up.

"In an age of such high pretensions to taste and knowledge, I trust these observations will meet with consideration.

"VIATOR ANTIQUARIUS."

EASTER SEPULCHRE.

A writer in the *Antiquarian and Topographical Cabinet* (vol. viii.) says of Bromley Church:—" The Sepulchral Memorials are numerous. Among these is an Ancient Tomb, in the north wall of the chancel, under a recessed pointed arch, with many mouldings springing from two beautifully slender pillars on each side, with heavy ornamented capitals. The upper portion of the arch and east side of the monument are mutilated. The person whose memory this tomb was intended to commemorate is unknown, but was conjectured by Weaver to be Richard Wendover, Bishop of Rochester, and Minister of this town; but this prelate, who died in 1250, was, according to Dart and Goodwin, buried in Westminster Abbey, by the King's (Henry III.) express orders."

Referring to this interesting object, Dr Beeby says:—" A small recess now on the north side of the altar, and originally situated beneath a small window in the north wall of the chancel, carries us back some five or six hundred years. Its foliated capitals and elegant mouldings have justly caused it to be described as a 'graceful relic of the Edwardian period.' There was formerly a hollow stone in its centre, the cavity being rectangular, and the entrance surrounded by a circular moulding. This cavity has been conjectured to have been the shrine of a heart; but its small size, only four inches by five, and the absence of any sufficient protection anteriorly, causes me to look upon this suggestion as doubtful, and to favour the supposition that the original use of the recess was that of a credence table."

The original position of this ornamental recess upon the north wall of the chancel is of itself significant, and may lead us to consider whether it may not have been an Easter Sepulchre. Such sepulchres were usually on the north side of the chancel, near the altar, as is the case in Bromley Church. Mr J. G. Waller, F.S.A., has given some interesting particulars of the ancient semi-dramatic service connected with the Easter Sepulchre, which will probably be useful in this connection.

"As many may not be acquainted with the nature of this ancient rite, I will endeavour in a few words to give an outline of its character. Although it approached very nearly to the mystery or miracle play, yet I think we may state as a distinction between them that whilst one was a popular drama on a religious subject, the other was a religious rite treated dramatically. A construction was made on the north side near the altar to simulate the sepulchre, and when tombs were erected, this was made upon them. On Good Friday, at the hour of Vespers, a crucifix, usually, doubtless, that from above the high altar, accompanied by the consecrated Host, was taken by the priest with ceremonious reverence, and placed in the sepulchre prepared. A watch was appointed to be by it by day and night until Easter Day, when, previous to the Mass, the clergy proceeded to the sepulchre, and removed the Crucifix and Host, and bore them to the altar again. The bell then rang out, and a service began with the singing of an antiphon, 'Christ is risen from the dead,' &c. Added to this, varying in many places, there was an impersonation of the Angels, the three Maries, the soldiers, &c.; and a dialogue took place between them, derived in a great measure from Scripture, or founded upon it. In point of fact, it was representing the sacred narrative, to render it popularly intelligible, on principles similar to those which dictated the symbolic character of ecclesiastical art."—*Surrey Archæological Collections*, vol. vii., pp. 69-70.

Parish Church Goods.

The following is a copy of an inventory of Parish Goods belonging to Bromley Church in the year 1552. The original document is preserved in the Record Office; but this copy is made from that which was printed in the eighth volume of *Archæologia Cantiana*.

Bromelly—XVI. November VI. Ed. VI.

William Momford and Richard Mathewe, churchwardens.
First one Crismatorye of silver being hole weyng xij ounces.
Item one pix of silver being hole xi ounces iij quarters.
Item ij cruetts of silver being hole .x. ounces.
Item one pax of sylver being hole vj ounces quarter.
Item one chalys of silver with his patent all gilt being hole weying xxij ounces di.
Item one other chalis with the patente of sylver parcell gylt being hole as it is waying xvj ounces di.

Item one other chalys with his patente of sylver parcell gylte being hole as it is waying ix ounces.
Item ij. crosses of copper with one fote of copper to the same.
Item one pix clothe of clothe of gold.
Item one canapie cloth of grene saten of bridges.
Item one cope of blewe velvett embrothered with aungells and starres of clothe of gold, & one sute of vestments to the same.
Item one cope of purple velvett embrothered with aungels spled egles and flowers.
Item one cope of chaungeable bawdkyn.
Item one cope of white satten of bridgs embrodered with flowers.
Item one vestment of blew velvet embrodered with flowers lakkyng an ames.
Item one cope of bawdekyn with a sute of vestments belonging to the same lakkying an albe and a stole.
Item one vestmente of blewe damaske embrodred with flowers.
Item one vestment of white satten.
Item one olde vestment of dornyx with an albe.
Item one vestment & an albe of blake satten of bridgs imbrodered with flowers.
Item one frunte clothe of tawney velvett with a border of clothe of golde and velvett perlede.
Item one frunt cloth of redd damaske embrodered with baudekyn.
Item one herse clothe of blake satten of bridgs with one crosse of redd satten of bridgs.
Item one frunt cloth of redd damaske.
Item ij frunt clothes of canvas paynted.
Item ij corporaxes & iij corporax casis.
Item v crosse & banner clothes of paynted lynnen clothe.

Item one holy water stokke of brasse.
Item iij olde latten basons, one dishe, & iiij cruetts of pewder.
Item ij sensers of copper, & one shippe of the same.
Item ij crosse staves half plated with copper.
Item iij latten candlestiks, & ij litle candelstiks of latten.
Item one pix of copper.
Item ij pix clothes thone of nedle work, thother of old redd silke.
Item one paire of organs.
Item ij curtens of yelowe and red saye for the quere.
Item ij towels thone of diaper thother of playne cloth.
Item v. surplesses of lynen clothe.
Item ij. great standardes of brasse.
Item one brasen lampe, & one hanging bason for the pastall.
Item one funt clothe of lynnen.
Item xx little bolles of pewder which did serve in the rode lofte.
Item one bible, and six alter clothes of lynnen.
Item iiij greate bells suted in the steple, one sants bell, and iij lytle sacrying bells, one hand bell, & ij olde alter pillowes.
Item one paraphrasis of Erasmus.
Item one lente vaile of lynnen clothe.
Item one booke of the homalies, & iij Englishe processioners.
Item xxxix s. ij d. remayning of a crosse of silver sold by the saide churchwardens.
Endorsed is a mem. made at Estgrenewich xvi November VI Ed VI that V olde Banner clothes and one crosse of silver and gilte waying LVI ounces were sold for xiiij li. vi^s ixd. of which all save xxxix^s ij d. has been layd out upon reparacyons of the churche.

Church Plate.

The Rev. A. G. Hellicar, Vicar of Bromley, has furnished an account of the church plate of Bromley Church to the recently issued seventeenth volume of "*Archæologia Cantiana.*" We take the liberty of transcribing from that account some particulars which we believe will be of interest to our readers. The Communion Vessels of Bromley Church are two Cups with their covers (1791 and 1807); two Patens (1796 and 1801); a Flagon (1817), a Spoon, or strainer, all of silver, and an Alms-dish of brass-gilt.

The silver gilt Cup, No. I., with its Paten-cover upon it, stands $10\frac{3}{4}$ inches high. Its bowl is $3\frac{7}{8}$ inches in diameter, and bears this inscription, "*Ecclesiá de Bromley (Comu. Cantii) furibus spoliatá, hoc proculum Cænæ Salvatoris nostri celebratione utendum, donavit Georgius Norman, ejusdem Parochiæ Generosus, Junii mense* A.D. MDCCXCI." The foot is $3\frac{3}{8}$ inches wide; the Cup and the Cover together weigh 1 lb. $6\frac{3}{4}$ ozs. The occasion for the gift of this Cup is narrated on the fly-leaf of a Parish Register, and printed in "*Archæologia Cantiana*," xiii., 164, as follows: "On the night of the 13th of April 1791, the vestry door was broken open, and the chest of deal in which the plate was kept was robbed of the following articles: 1 large flaggon, with lid fixt, 1 quart Chalice, 1 rich chased Chalice and loose cover, with a straining spoon, 1 large paten, and 1 small paten. The above were all gilt."

The silver Cup, No. II., with its Paten-cover, together stand 11 inches high. The bowl, 4 inches in diameter, is inscribed, "*Bromley, Kent,* 1807 | *Henry Smith, D.D.*, Minister | *Robert Smith, senr.*, | *Christopher Fisher,* Churchwardens." The diameter of the foot of this Cup is 3½ inches. The total weight of Cup and Cover together is 1 lb. 10¾ ozs. Upon the Paten Cover is engraved the sacred monogram IHS, with cross and nails, all *en soleil*.

Silver Gilt Paten, No. I., 9½ inches in diameter, weighs 13¼ ozs. It is engraved, like Paten-cover, No. II., with the sacred monogram *en soleil*, and has also these words, "*The gift of Robert Makepeace for the use of the Communion Table in Bromley Church*, 1803."

Silver Gilt Paten, No. II., 9¾ inches in diameter, weighs 16 ozs. It bears the sacred monogram and the inscription similar to those on Paten No. I.

The silver Flagon, gilt inside, stands 12 inches high, and weighs 3 lbs. 11¼ ozs. Its cylindrical body is 4⅜ inches in diameter; its splayed foot is 7 inches wide. It bears this inscription, "*James Edward Newell, M.A., gave this Flagon to the Church of Bromley, March* 10*th*, 1854."

The silver gilt Spoon, or strainer, is 8⅞ inches long, and weighs 2½ ozs. It is inscribed, "*Bromley Parish.*"

The gilt brass Alms-dish, 15⅞ inches in diameter, weighs 2 lbs. 5½ ozs; it bears this inscription, "*Presented to the Parish Church of Bromley, Kent, by Evelyn Arthur, Mabel Katrine, and Sydenham Malthus Hellicar, May* 1873;" and also this text, "*It is more blessed to give than to receive.*" The donors of this dish are the children of the Vicar.

It may be stated that the Communion Table in Bromley Church is formed of roughly worked oak, and may date from a period soon after the Reformation.

Bells.

The curious custom of ringing the Pancake Bell on Shrove Tuesday is still observed at Bromley Church, although the reason for it is probably well-nigh forgotten. A tradition affirms that the ringer of the bell was supposed to be entitled to receive one pancake from each house in the town. The original purpose of ringing the bell was to call the parishioners to the church, where the priest sat in an open chair, or stall, to hear the confessions of his people, to award them such penance as he thought good for them, or to give them absolution. The week preceding Lent was an appropriate time for all to perform that duty. It was for that reason called Shrove-tide, and the Tuesday in it was formerly and still is known as Shrove, Shrive, or Confession Tuesday. On Shrove Tuesday, we are told by a writer in *Notes and Queries*, the housewives, in order to use up all the grease, lard, dripping, etc., made pancakes, and the apprentices and others about the house were summoned to the meal by the ringing of a bell (probably by the ringing of the confession bell), which was for that reason denominated the Pancake Bell. The ringing of the Pancake Bell is still continued in many churches throughout the kingdom, and it is not a little extraordinary that the custom should have survived for so many years the purpose which first gave rise to it.

The following are the inscriptions upon the bells of Bromley Church:—

I. Prosperity to the Parish of Bromley.
   T. Janaway Fecit 1773.

II. Musica est Mentis Medicina.
    Thomas Janaway Fecit 1773.

III. HE AND HE ONLY AIMS ARIGHT WHO JOYNS
INDUSTRY WITH DELIGHT.
THOS. JANAWAY FECIT 1773.

IV. WHEN FROM THE EARTH OUR NOTES REBOUND
THE HILLS AND VALLEYS ECCO ROUND.
THOS. JANAWAY FECIT 1773.

V. THOS. JANAWAY FECIT 1773.

VI. THOMAS JANAWAY FECIT 1773.

VII. THE RINGERS ART OUR GRATEFUL NOTES
PROLONG
APOLLO LISTENS AND APROVES THE SONG.
THOMAS JANAWAY FECIT 1773.

VIII. JOSEPH SHIRLEY & IOHN MANN CHURCH
WARDENS 1773.
THOMAS JANAWAY FECIT.

Sanctus. THOMAS JANAWAY FECIT 1777.

It may be mentioned that Mr Stahlschmidt, in his recent book on "The Church Bells of Kent," speaks of Thomas Janaway, the founder of the Bromley bells, as a Chelsea man, and, further, he says "his works are of good quality." It seems he founded bells for the following churches:—Bexley, Blackheath, Brasted, Great Mongeham, and Knockholt.

The following is an interesting extract from the Ringers' Book: "The first peal on the eight bells of Bromley Church was performed on the 14th day of September 1774, which consisted of 5040 Changes of Bob Major, and was completed in 3 hours and 14 minutes.

BROMLEY.

Names of the Ringers.

John Cowdery,
John Chapman, Jun.,
John Day,
John Heath,
Henry Sale,
Thomas Kelly,
William Chapman,
William Cook."

The following is from Hone's "Table Book," Vol. ii., pp. 527-530:—

"I stept into 'The Sun—R. Tape,' at Bromley, to make inquiry of the landlord respecting a stage to London; and, over the parlour mantelpiece, carefully glazed, in gilt frame, beneath the flourishing surmounting scroll, there appeared the following inscription *in letters of gold*":—

Rang at St Peters Bromley.

On the 15th January, 1817, by the Society of Bromley Youths, A complete Peal of *Grandsire Triples*, which is 5040 changes with the *Bells Muffled*, in commemoration of Wm. Chapman deceased, being a Ringer in the Parish of Bromley 43 years, and rang upwards of 60 peals. This Dumb Peal was completed in 3 hours and 6 minutes.

Thos. Giles............ 1st	Wm. King 5th
Rd. Chapman......... 2nd	Jno. Allen 6th
Wm. Sanger 3rd	Wm. Fuller............7th
Ge. Stone 4th	Jno. Green............8th

Being the first Dumb Peal of this kind ever rang in this kingdom, and conducted by J. Allen.

Church-Door.

In Hone's "Table Book," Vol. ii., p. 97, there is an engraving of the old door of Bromley Church, and on page 101 of the same volume a representation is given of the ancient key belonging to the same edifice. In addition to the engravings there are about five columns of entertaining matter relating to the same subject. We select the following as useful for our purpose.

"On our visit to Bromley church, as soon as the modern outer gates of the porch were unlocked, we were struck by the venerable appearance of the old inner oak door; and, instead of taking a view of the church, of which there are several prints, Mr Williams made a drawing of the decayed portal, from whence he executed the present engraving. On the hinge-side of the engraving, there is a representation of the outer edge of the door.

"This door formerly hung on the western stone jamb; but, for warmth, and greater convenience, the churchwardens, under whose management the edifice was last repaired, put up a pair of folding-doors, covered with crimson cloth; yet with a respectful regard, worthy of imitation in other places, they preserved this vestige of antiquity, and were even careful to display its time-worn front. For this purpose the door has been attached to the eastern jamb, so that if it were shut its ornamental side would be hidden; instead whereof, it is kept open by a slight fastening against the eastern form, within the porch . . . Bromley Church-door is a vestige; for on examination it will be found not perfect. It is seven feet four inches in height, and in width four feet eight inches; the width of the doorway, between the stone jambs, is two inches more; the width of the door itself, therefore, has been reduced these two inches; and hence the centre of the ornaments in relief is not in the centre of the door in its present state. It is a good specimen of the fast-decaying and often prematurely-removed, fine doors of our old churches. The lock, probably of like age with the door, and also of wood, is a massive effectual contrivance, two feet six inches long, seven inches and a half deep, and five inches thick; with a bolt an inch in height, and an inch and a half in thickness, that shoots out two inches on the application of the rude heavy key."

John Weever tells us very little about Bromley Church in his " Ancient Funerall Monuments," printed in 1631. The following is what he says:—

"*Bromley.*

"In the Church wall lyeth the pourtraiture, as I learne by tradition, of *Richard Wendoucr*, Bishop of Rochester, and Parson of this Towne. He was consecrated 1238, and dyed 1250, yet it is said, that his body was buried in Westminster by the kings special commandement, for that he was accounted a very holy and vertuous man: which I cannot much contradict.

"*Icy gist Mestre Water de Henche,*
Qi fut Persone de Bromleghe.   1360."

This interesting monument has long since disappeared. Even Thorpe does not appear to have seen it, as, although he quotes the inscription in his "*Registrum Roffense*," he does so without any remark as to its position in the church.

BRASSES.

The following are the inscriptions upon the monumental brasses in Bromley Church, arranged in chronological order.

Brass affixed to the north wall of the chancel.

Hic iacet Isabella qndā vr̃ Ricī Lacer nuper Maior Londōn que obiit qrto kl. Augt ā dī M.CCCLXI cui' aīe ppiciet deus ām

This brass was for many years lost, but in the repairs which Bromley Church underwent in 1829, it was found again, see *Gentleman's Magazine*, March 1830, p. 208.

Brass on the floor of the nave.

I DO MOST ASSVREDLY BELIEVE
THAT MY REDEMER LIVETH.

HERE LYETH BVRIED THE BODIE OF RICHARD THORNHILL LATE OF BROMLYE IN THE COVNTYE OF KENT ESQ: WHO DECEASED THE XVTH DAY OF FEBRVARYE 1600. WHO FIRST MARRIED MARGARET MILLS AND HAD ISSVE BY HER TWO SONNES AND THREE DAVGHTERS: AND AFTERWARDS MARRYED ELIZABETH WATSON AND HAD ISSVE BY HER TWO SONNES AND ONE DAVGHTER.

This is a fine brass about six feet in length, and three feet in breadth, with arms and effigies. The figure of Richard Thornhill is nearly three feet in length. He has a short frill, long cloak with extra-long sleeves hanging at his sides. He wears a close-cropped beard and moustache. The figure of the lady on his left-hand side is about two feet ten inches in length. She is represented as being attired in a high frill, stiff head-dress, and a dress with full skirt, and close-fitting body ornamented with a curiously interlaced pattern. The figure of the lady on the right-hand side is unfortunately mutilated. What remains of the figure is about two feet in length, being the lower part of the effigy. The costume of this lady appears to be similar to that of the lady first mentioned. All the effigies are shown with clasped hands.

Brass on the floor of the nave.

HERE VNDER LYETH BVRIED THE BODYE
OF MR JOHN KING OF LONDON DRAPER
AND FREE OF THE COMPANY OF CLOTH
WORKERS WHO DEPARTED THIS WORLDE
THE FIFTE OF SEPTEMBER ANNO DŌM 1603
ÆTATIS SVI LI
HE HAD TO WIFE SVSAN WOODWARDE
BY WHOM HE LEFTE ISSVE THEN LIVINGE
HENRY, IAMES, IOHN AND ELIZABETH.

Brass on the floor of the nave, near the pulpit.

MEMORIÆ SACRVM
IOANNI YONGE EPISCOPO ROFFENSI SACRÆ
THEOLOGIÆ DOCTORI LONDINI NATO CAN
TABRIGIÆ BONIS LITERIS INNVTRITO
NON MINVS VARIA DOCTRINA & PRVDEN
TIA, QVAM VITÆ SANCTIMONIA CLARO
QVI CVM DOMINO DIV VIGILASSET SE
NEX IN DOMINO PIE PLACIDEQ OBDORMI
VIT DIE X APRILIS MDCV CVM ANNOS
XXVII SEDISSET EPISCOPVS & LXXI VIXISSET.

Brass on the floor of the nave.

HERE LYETH YE BODY OF IANE BODENHAM YE DAVGHTER OF IOHN BREW-
TON OF SOUTHWARK GENT: & WIFE TO HENRY BODENHAM OF FOLSTON IN
YE COVNTY OF WILTSHIRE ESQR BY WHOM SHE HAD ISSVE 1 DAVGHTER & 2
SONES, ANN, PHILLIP, & IOHN, SHEE DIED YE 12 OF NOVR 1625 AT YE AGE
OF XXI.

ME, NVPTVS, NATVS, FRATER, MATERVE, PATERVE,
ORBAM NON PLORENT, ORBIS : ASTRA FEROR.
SE, NVPTVS, NATVS, FRATER, MATERQ PATERQ,
ORBIBVS ASTRORVM DEFLEAT ORBVS AD HVC.
DVM, NVPTVM, NATOS, FRATREM, MATREMQ PATREMQ
QVERO : BEAT SOCIAM, NATA, BEATA, MATREM.

Brass inserted in the masonry of the south pier of the chancel arch.

> HERE LYETH BVRIED THE BODYE
> OF IOHN MAVNSELL SOMETYME
> OF CHICHELY IN THE COVNTY OF
> BVCKINGHAM ESQVIER. HE HAD
> ISSVE TWO SONNES, IOHN AND
> THOMAS AND DEPARTED THIS
> LIFE THE 19 DAY OF OCTOBER
> ANNO DOM 1625 BEINGE ABOVT
> THE AGE OF 50 YEARS.

In Thorpe's "*Registrum Roffense*," the following lines are given as a final part of the inscription :—

> "Short was his life, yet dyes he never;
> Death has his due, yet lives he ever."

MONUMENTS.

The monumental inscriptions within the walls of Bromley Church are numerous, and in a local and limited sense, of great interest; but it is doubted whether that interest is sufficiently general to justify the insertion in this place of complete transcripts of the whole of them. One or two of the inscriptions, however, are of world-wide interest.

In March 1752, Elizabeth, the wife of the celebrated Samuel Johnson died, and her remains were brought to Bromley and deposited at the western end of the nave. Boswell, in his "*Life of Johnson*," mentions that Bromley was probably fixed upon because of the residence there of Johnson's friend Hawkesworth. A few months before his death Johnson made arrangements for placing a memorial over the remains of his wife, and he wrote the following letter to Rev. T. Bagshaw, the clergyman of Bromley :

"Sir, Perhaps you may remember that in the year 1753, you committed to the ground my dear wife. I now intreat your permission to lay a stone upon her, and have sent the inscription, that if you find it proper you may signify your allowance.

"You will do me a great favour by showing the place where she lies, that the stone may protect her remains. Mr Ryland will wait upon you for the inscription and procure it to be engraved: you will easily believe that I shrink from this mournful office; when it is done, if I have strength remaining, I will visit Bromley once again, and pay you part of the respect to which you have a right from,

"Reverend Sir, your most humble servant,

"Sam Johnson."

Arrangements were made accordingly, and a plain flat ledger stone was placed over the grave of Mrs Johnson in Bromley Church, where it still remains. The following is the inscription which it bears:

Hic conduntur reliquiæ
ELIZABETHÆ
Antiquâ Jarvisiorum gente,
Peatlingæ, apud Leicestrienses, ortæ;
Formosæ, cultæ, ingeniosæ, piæ,
Uxoris, primis nuptiis, Henrici Porter,
Secundis, Samuelis Johnson:
Qui multum amatam diuque defletam
Hoc lapide contexit.
Obiit Londini, Mense Mart,
A.D. MDCCLIII.

It will be observed that both in Johnson's letter, quoted above, and in the inscription, the year of Mrs Johnson's death is stated to be 1753, whereas we know upon the best authority, that it took place in 1752. There is no doubt that Dr Johnson made the error when he composed the epitaph for his wife's gravestone a short time before his death, which, we may add, did not occur until upwards of thirty years after that of his wife.

On the south wall of the chancel is a marble monument, with armorial and other enrichments, to the memory of Zachary Pearce, Bishop of Rochester. The inscription is well worthy of note as showing the rapidity with which various preferments were showered upon him.

"In the South Isle lyeth the body of
ZACHARY PEARCE, D.D.
Who was made Rector of St Bartholomew's behind
the Royal Exchange, London, March 10th, 1720,
Vicar of St Martin's in the Fields Westminster
January the 10th 1724,
Dean of WINCHESTER, August the 4th 1739,
Prolocutor of the LOWER HOUSE of Convocation
December 7th, 1744,
Bishop of BANGOR February 21st, 1748,
Dean of WESTMINSTER May 4th, 1756,
And Bishop of ROCHESTER June 4th, 1756.
He resigned the Deanery of WESTMINSTER
June 24th 1768,
And Died in a comfortable hope of (what was
the chief aim of all his Labours upon Earth)
The being promoted to a happier Place in Heaven.
He was Born September the 8th, 1690.
And Died June 29th 1774. Aged 84 years.

In the same Vault is interred
Mrs. MARY PEARCE
wife of ZACHARY
Lord Bishop of ROCHESTER
who died October 23rd 1773
Aged 70 years."

In the south gallery of the church the following curious inscription occurs:—

"Sacred to the memory of
Thomas Chase, Esq., formerly of this parish, born in the city of Lisbon, the 1st of November, 1729, and buried under the ruins of the same house where he first saw the light, in the ever memorable and terrible earthquake which befell that city on the 1st of November, 1755, when, after a most wonderful escape, he, by degrees, recovered from a very deplorable condition, lived till the 20th November, 1788, aged 59 years."

In Freeman's "History of the Parish of Bromley," it is stated that Mr Chase resided at a house on Bromley Common.

For several years Dr Hawkesworth lived in an old house at Bromley, where his wife kept a boarding-school. The house was that in which the families of Knight and Thornhill had formerly dwelt.

Hawkesworth, about the year 1744, became Samuel Johnson's successor in the office of compiler of the parliamentary debates for the *Gentleman's Magazine*. Indeed there was a close friendship between these two literary characters, and during its continuance Mrs Johnson died, and was buried at Bromley. After Hawkesworth received the honour of LL.D., however, a coldness seems to have arisen between him and Johnson, and it is said that this was owing to Johnson's jealousy of his friend's distinction. Hawkesworth was buried at Bromley, and his monument is in the north gallery, bearing the following inscription:—

" To the memory of
John Hawkesworth, LL.D.,
who died the 17th of November, 1773, aged 57 years. That he lived ornamental and useful to society, in an eminent degree, was among the boasted felicities of the present age; that he laboured for the benefit of posterity, let his own pathetic admonition at once record and realize.

" *From the Adventurer,* No. 140.

" The hour approaches in which whatever praise I have acquired by these compositions will be remembered with indifference, and the tenour of them alone will afford me comfort. Time, who is impatient to date my last paper, will shortly moulder the hand that is now writing it in the dust, and still the heart that now throbs at the reflection. But let not this be read as something that relates only to another; a few years only can divide the eye that is reading from the hand that has written this awful truth. However obvious, and however reiterated, it is frequently forgotten; for surely if we did not lose our remembrance, or at least our sensibility, that alone would always predominate in our lives which alone can afford us comfort when we die." [1]

" *Bromley in Kent, March* 8, 1754."

[1] It may be remarked that this extract from the "*Adventurer*" differs considerably from what Dr Hawkesworth originally wrote. It appears to have been subsequently altered by some one, or taken from a later edition of the "*Adventurer*."

The following epitaph in memory of Elizabeth Monk, is placed upon the external east wall of the Church. It was written by Dr Hawkesworth:—

"Near this place lies the body of
ELIZABETH MONK,
who departed this life on the 27th day of August, 1753, aged 101. She was the widow of John Monk, late of this parish, blacksmith, her second husband, to whom she had been a wife near fifty years, by whom she had no children, and of the issue of the first marriage none lived to the second. But virtue would not suffer her to be childless: an infant, to whom and to whose father she had been nurse (such is the uncertainty of temporal prosperity), became dependent upon strangers for the necessaries of life; to him she afforded the protection of a mother. This parental charity was returned with filial affection; and she was supported in the feebleness of age, by him whom she had cherished in the helplessness of infancy. Let it be remembered that there is no station in which industry will not obtain power to be liberal, nor any character on which liberality will not confer honour. She had long been prepared by a simple and unaffected piety for that awful moment, which however delayed, is universally sure. How few are allowed an equal time to probation? How many by their lives appear to presume upon more? To preserve the memory of this person, and yet more to perpetuate the lesson of her life, this stone was erected by voluntary contributions."

Benefactions to the Parish.

"The value and uses of the public charities and benefactions in the parish of Bromley, together with the names of the several benefactors:—

"The right reverend John Warner, lord bishop of Rochester, founded the College for the support and maintenance of twenty widows of loyall and orthodox clergymen, and a chaplain. The yearly salary of every widow he appointed to be twenty pounds, that of the chaplain fifty. Sir Orlando Bridgeman and Sir Philip Warwick, two of the bishop's executors, left one hundred pounds each towards the repairs of the building; and the reverend Dr Plume, archdeacon of this diocese, another hundred pounds for the benefit of the widows.

"The right reverend John Buckeridge, lord bishop of Ely, did by his last will and testament give and bequeath the sum of twenty pounds, to be employed for some yearly benefit for the poor of this parish, with which, and the addition of some little money beside, a purchase was made of a house in Nichol-lane, rented at forty shillings a year; which sum, necessary repairs being first deducted, is to be distributed every Good Friday (or near that time) amongst the poorest and most necessitous inhabitants.

"The reverend George Wilson, late rector of Chislehurst, did at his death leave the sum of two hundred pounds, to be disposed off in a purchase, the annual income of which he directed to be appropriated to the sole use and benefit of the charity school for ever."—*Registrum Roffense.*

The following additional charities are noted by Hasted :—

Jasper Greene, vicar of Woodnesborough, by his will in 1660, gave 20s. yearly to the poor of this parish.

Dr John Warner, bishop of Rochester, bequeathed by his will £20 in money, for the benefit of the poor of this parish.

Parish Registers.

The Parish Registers, &c., of Bromley, date from the following years:—

   Register of Baptisms, 1558.
   Register of Marriages, 1575.
   Register of Burials, 1578.
   Churchwardens' Accounts, 1673.

Lysons quotes the following entries from the Registers as worthy of note:—

"The 14 of Maye the reverend father, John, Byshop of Rochester, had his funeral solemnized, his sonne, Mr. John Younge, being cheefe mourner, 1605."

"May 31, 1631—the Rt. Revd. Father in God, John Buckeridge, the Ld. Bishop of Ely, sometime Bishop of Rochester, buried."

"George, son of Sr George Jeffreys, Knt, Recorder of London, buried Aug. 26, 1679."

"Joseph, Benjamin, and Rachel, children of John Dudley, baptized Oct. 17, buried Oct. 20, 1724."

"Elizabeth Monk, widow, aged 101 last April, buried Sept. 3, 1753."

"Mary White, widow, aged 100, buried Jan. 9, 1800."

A fly-leaf of the Register Book bears the following memorandum in the handwriting of Dr Henry Smith, the vicar of the Parish.

"On the night of the 13th of April of this year, 1791, the vestry-room door was broken open, and the chest of deal, in which the plate was kept, was robbed of the following articles; one large flagon, with lid fixt; one quart chalice, one rich chased chalice and loose cover, with a straining spoon, one large paten, and one small paten; the above were all gilt; the gold fringe from the pulpit and communion hangings; one large damask table cloth, and two damask napkins.

"It appears, from every observation, that the perpetrators of this sacrilegious deed must have secreted themselves in the Church during the morning service, for there were not the least traces of violence upon the doors, walls, or windows; they let themselves out of the Church by unscrewing the locks of the doors leading to the gallery at the east end of the Church, which must have been done on the inside.

"A bottle of Tent wine was taken out of the cupboard and drunk; which makes me think there were more than one, and indeed I can hardly imagine *one* person to have courage sufficient to carry him through such a Diabolical Enterprize.

"Hy. Smith, Minister."

In 1733 Peter Kelk gave to Bromley Parish a black cloth pall, trimmed with white sarcenet. The poor were to have the free use of it, but those who could afford to do so were expected to pay a certain sum for the privilege. The money thus collected was distributed by the churchwardens to the deserving poor every Christmas Day in the Church porch.

BROMLEY.

RECTORS AND VICARS.

Rectors.

    Richard de Wendover, 1226 to 1238, afterwards Bishop of Rochester, died 1250, buried in Westminster Abbey. Cenotaph monument formerly in Bromley Church. *See Weever.*

    John Sudbury, in the reign of Henry III.

    Abel de Sancto Martino, 1292.

    William de Bliburg, 1310. (?)

    John de Frendesburie deprived, 1329, by the Bishop of Rochester for disobedience, the Bishop placed Hugh de Penebregge in his room; notwithstanding which, it is said, that Frendesburie thrust him out by force.

    Hugh de Penebregge, collated 1329.

    Walter de Henche, afterwards Bishop of Rochester, died 1360. Buried in Bromley Church.

    William Fryston.

    Richard Fryston, 1456.

    ———— Wymando, 1465.

    Emery Tulfelde, 1537.

Vicars.

    James Dyer, 1604.

    Stephen Constantine, 1607.

    John Preston, 1608.

    Jasper Greene, 1620.

    William Wallis, died 1624.

    John Hodges, 1627.

    Noah Webb, 1628.

    Robert Rainsford, 1630.

Richard Rathbone, 1634.
Thomas Smith, died 1639.
Robert Antrobus, 1640.
Jasper Jackson, 1647.
Henry Arnold, 1654; one of the 2000 ministers ejected for nonconformity by the Bartholomew Act.
Joseph March, 1663.
Thomas Pike, 1666.
Daniel Barton, 1667.
Edmund Lee, 1670.
S. Grascombes, 1681.
William Wilson, 1682; afterwards Rector of Chislehurst.
Thomas Johnson, 1684.
Edward Roman, 1686.
Henry Maundrell, 1690.
Samuel Bowles, 1695.
Harrington Bagshaw, 1698, died 1759; also Rector of Woolwich and Chaplain of Bromley College.
Joseph Sims, 1739.
Thomas Bagshaw, 1744, died 1787; also Rector of Southfleet and Chaplain of Bromley College.
Henry Smith, D.D., 1785, died 1818.
John Baker, M.A., 1818, resigned 1820.
Walker King, M.A., instituted for about three months in 1826.
James Edward Newell, M.A., 1820, resigned 1865.
Arthur Gresley Hellicar, M.A., 1865, the present Vicar.

The Rectory.

The site upon which the rectory-house formerly stood is near the churchyard. A rectory is described as having existed in the reign of Charles I., which, according to Hasted's account, consisted of "a manor and good mansion house with a gate house and large tithe barn, with eleven bayes and two small barns and fifty-one acres of glebe land." The living of Bromley was originally a rectory, and the rectors used to hold courts and summon and fine those of their parishioners and tenants who failed to pay their dues. There is still preserved a record of such courts held by Richard Fryston, clerk, in the reign of Henry VI., 1454. In the year 1287, the rectory was rated at 30 marks; in 1534, at £39. 12s. The living of Bromley continued a rectory until the year 1537, when, by order of Henry VIII., it was transferred to the Bishops of Rochester, who were commanded to "appoint, ordain, and sufficiently endow perpetual vicars," also to "cause to be distributed a certain reasonable sum of money, arising from the fruits of the Church of Bromley, among the poor parishioners of the aforesaid Church in each ensuing year for ever." (Patent Rolls, Henry VIII. Extract in possession of C. Child, Esq. Quoted by Dr Beeby.)

"The rectorial manor, parsonage-house, glebe-land, and tithes were valued all together, in the year 1650, at £182. 8s. 9d. per annum. They had been all leased by Bishop Warner for 21 years, commencing in 1639, at the reserved rent of £60 per ann. and 40 quarters of oats. John Younge was lessee in 1646. In 1706, the lease was in the possession of William Emmett, Esq., whose granddaughter brought it to Mr John Innocent. In 1811, George Norman, Esq., was lessee, whose father married Mr Innocent's daughter." (*Lysons*.) The great tithes are now in the hands of the Ecclesiastical Commissioners.

Since the appropriation of the rectory it appears to have been usual to grant leases both of the tithes and glebe land; also of the Church House, which latter was rebuilt at the commencement of the 18th century. In 1868, this house being still let on lease, a vicarage was built by subscription to supply the urgent need of a parsonage near the Church.

Parish Umbrella.

Hone, in his *Table Book*, Vol. 2, pp. 101-2, says, "I particularly noticed a capital large umbrella of old construction, which I brought out and set up in the church-yard; with its wooden handle, fixed into a movable shaft, shod with an iron point at the bottom, and struck into the ground. It stood seven feet high; the awning is of a green-oiled canvass, such as common umbrellas were made of forty years ago, and is stretched on ribs of cane. It opens to a diameter of five feet, and forms a decent and capacious covering for the Minister whilst engaged in the burial-service at the grave. It is in every respect a more fitting exhibition than the watch-box sort of vehicle devised for the same purpose, and in some church-yards trundled from grave to grave, wherein the Minister and Clerk stand, like the ordinary of Newgate, and a dying malefactor at the new drop in the Old Bailey. An unseemly thing of this description is used at St George's in the Borough."

Funereal Garland.

In the year 1733, a very curious and valuable funeral garland was dug up in Bromley Churchyard by the Parish Clerk then in office.

It is described so well in the *Gentleman's Magazine* for 1747, and accompanied by so many useful remarks that we shall make no apology for introducing the whole of the article in this place.

"Of Burial Garlands.

"Sir,—Being a constant reader of your instructive, as well as diverting Magazine, I take the liberty to present you with some remarks on a passage of that in *December* last, p. 646, which gives an account of an hour-glass found in a grave in *Clerkenwell Church-yard;* and that some antiquarians supposed, that it was an ancient custom to put an hour glass into the coffin, as an emblem of the sand of life being run out; others conjectured that little hour glasses were anciently given at funerals, like rosemary, and by the friends of the dead put in the coffin or the grave.

"But I fear neither of these customs can be prov'd by the works of any authentic author; besides, had such been the use or custom, certainly these glasses, or at least fragments of them, would be more frequently discovered. Give me leave, Sir, therefore, to offer what I flatter myself will seem a more probable reason for the hour glass's interment.

"In this nation (as well as others) by the abundant zeal of our ancestors, virginity was held in great estimation; insomuch that those which died in that state were rewarded at their deaths, with a garland or crown on their heads, denoting their triumphant victory over the lusts of the flesh. Nay, this honour was extended even to a widow that had enjoy'd but one husband (saith *Weaver* in his *Fun. Mon.* p. 12). And in the year 1733, the present clerk of the parish church of *Bromley, in Kent,* by his digging a grave in that churchyard, close to the east end of the chancel wall, dug up one of those crowns or garlands, which is most artificially wrought in filagree work in gold and silver wire, in resemblance of myrtle (with which plant the funebrial garlands of the ancients were compos'd,[1]) whose leaves are fasten'd to hoops of larger wire of iron, now something crowded with rust, but both the gold and silver remains to this time very little different from its original splendour. It was also lin'd with cloth of silver, a piece of which, together with part of this curious garland, I keep as a choice relick of antiquity.

"Besides these crowns the ancients had also their depository garlands, the use of which were continued even till of late years (and perhaps are still retain'd in many parts of this nation, for my own knowledge of these matters extends not above 20 or 30 miles round *London*), which garlands, at the funereals of the deceas'd, were carried solemnly before the corps by two maids, and afterwards hung up in some conspicuous place within the church, in memorial of the departed person, and were (at least all that I have seen) made after the following manner, viz., the lower rim or circlet, was a broad hoop of wood, whereunto were fix'd, at the sides thereof, part of two other hoops crossing each other at the top, at right angles, which formed the upper part, being about one third longer than the width. These hoops were wholly covered with artificial flowers of paper, dy'd horn, or silk, and more or less beauteous, according to the skill or ingenuity of the performer. In the vacancy of the inside, from the top, hung white paper, cut in form of gloves, whereon was wrote deceased's name, age, &c., together with long slips of various-colour'd paper or ribbons. These were many times intermix'd with gilded or painted empty shells of blown eggs, as farther ornaments; or, it may be, as emblems of the bubbles

[1] See Thos. Brown's *Misc. Tracts*, p. 29.

and bitterness of this life; whilst other garlands had only a solitary hour-glass hanging therein, as a more significant symbol of mortality.

"About 40 years ago these garlands grew much out of repute, and were thought by many as very unbecoming decorations for so sacred a place as the church; and at the reparation, or new beautifying several churches where I have been concern'd, I was oblig'd by order of the minister and church-wardens, to take the garlands down, and the inhabitants strictly forbid to hang up any more for the future. Yet, notwithstanding, several people, unwilling to forsake their ancient and delightful custom, continued still the making of them, and they were carried at the funerals as before, to the grave, and put therein upon the coffin, over the face of the dead. This I have seen done in many places.

"Now, I doubt not but such a garland, with an hour-glass, was thus placed in the grave at *Clerkenwell*, which, at the rotting and falling in of the lid of the coffin, must consequently be so close to the skull as that was said to be, and the wooden frame of the glass being but of slender substance, must needs have been long since decay'd, had it not been in great measure secured from moisture within the hollow part of the garland, tho' the thread that held it might in a short time let it slip down to the coffin's lid.

"Thus, Sir, I have given my thoughts of your *Clerkenwell* hour-glass, altho' there may be several things found in graves not so easily accounted for. As in digging a grave, *Anno* 1720, for one Mr *Will. Clements, in Knockholt* churchyard in this country were found deep in the earth several rolls of brimstone; and last year was dug out of a grave at *Wilmington*, near *Dartford*, a quantity of *Henry* the III'ds. coins, the particular account of which I intend shall be the subject of another letter, if it will be any ways entertaining or acceptable to your readers, the which will be a great pleasure to,

"SIR, *your most obedient,*

"E. S."

"*Bromley, in Kent.*"

RAVENSCROFT.

Ravenscroft is a picturesque house situated on Masons Hill, and is the property of E. Soames, Esq. The front of the house bears the date 1660, which is probably the year of its erection. The north front is original work, but some parts of the house have been altered during the last 30 years. An old stone mantelpiece in the house, decorated with grapes carved in slight relief, has been referred to Elizabeth's period.

THE "BULL INN."

Numbers 6, 7, and 8, Market Square, were formerly used as an inn, and bore the sign first of "The Bull," and afterwards of "The King and Queen." We mention this house chiefly for the purpose of drawing attention to some remarkably interesting painted panels with which the walls of one room therein are decorated. The room belongs to that part of the house which is now in the occupation of Mr Heaysman, and is situated upon the ground floor, close by the butcher's shop. The paintings are of various sizes, and about thirty in number. The subjects represented are landscapes, maritime views, ships, &c., and also cut blossoms in baskets. Mr Edward Isard, to whom the house belongs, has kindly informed me that he possesses some documents from which it appears that the paintings are about 200 years old. The exact date of the paintings and the artist's name are not known. There is one long room in the front of the house, upon the first floor, for the accommodation, no doubt, of large assemblies during the time the house was used as an inn, and, although now separated, it can be thrown open into one room at pleasure. My best thanks are due to Mr Heaysman for courteously showing me the paintings, and to Mr Isard for the above information.

Bromley Tokens.

The following are the inscriptions upon five seventeenth-century tokens issued at Bromley.

Obv. Thomas . Ghost . at . the = (*A Hart lodged.*) ½d.
Rev. In . Bromley . in . Kent = his half peny.

Obv. Robert . Kinge . in = (*Two Keys Crossed.*) ¼d.
Rev. Bromley . in . Kent = R.M.K.

Obv. Michaell . (Lee ye White?) = (*A Hart lodged.*) ¼d.
Rev. In Brvmley . 1664 = M E.L.

Obv. John Percivall . of . 1667 = (*A roll of tobacco.*) ½d.
Rev. Brvmley . His . Half . Peny = I.E.P.

Obv. William . Waldron . of . Brvmly = (*A man making candles.*)
Rev. In . Kent . His . Half . Penny = W.A.W. ½d.

Proclamation of James II.

The following entry in Evelyn's "Diary," under the date of Feb. 10th, 1685, relates to the proclamation of James II. at Bromley:—

"Being sent to by the Sheriff of the County to appeare and assist in proclayming the King, I went the next day to Bromley, where I met the Sheriff and the Commander of the Kentish Troop, with an appearance, I suppose, of about 500 horse, and innumerable people, two of his Ma$^{ty's}$ trumpets and a Sergeant with other officers, who having drawn up the horse in a large field neere the towne, march'd thence, with swords drawne, to the market-place, where making a ring, after sound of trumpets and silence made, the High Sheriff read the proclaiming titles to his bailiffe, who repeated them aloud, and then after many shouts of the people, his Ma$^{ty's}$ health being drunk in a flint glass of a yard long, by the Sheriff, Commander, Officers, and cheife Gentlemen, they all dispers'd, and I return'd."

Old Market House.

The old Market House formerly stood in the Market Square, where the Town Hall now stands. It was a picturesque building, as will be seen from the vignette representation of it on the title-page of this volume. The lower part of it was used for the weekly market every Thursday. In the room above were held the meetings of the Commissioners of the Court of Requests, who assembled and heard cases every Thursday. It was also often hired for sales by auction. In 1858 the Market House, no longer used as a market, was used as an upholsterer's warehouse. In 1865 it was pulled down, and the present Town Hall was built in its place.

The market was granted to the Bishop of Rochester in the 25th and 26th years of Henry VI., to be held weekly within his manor of Bromley. At the end of the last century it was much resorted to for the sale of corn, live cattle, and every kind of provisions. It is now chiefly a mart for the sale of every description of cheap wearing apparel, crockery, provisions, and other miscellaneous articles. Two fairs were granted at the same time, one to be held on the feast of St James the Apostle, and the other on the day of St Blaze.

WIDMORE.

The name of this place was anciently written Wigmore, Windemere, Wymere, and Wyndemere. The name may perhaps be derived from the Anglo-Saxon Wig = war, and Moor = waste ground, although other derivations may be equally probable.

There is an ancient picturesque cottage at Widmore, with a gateway upon which are the initials and date, "A. B., 1559." Dr Beeby records the following interesting facts in connection with it. There is, in the possession of Miss Ellis, an engraving of the place, executed in 1714, in which a notice hangs from the arch, "J. Curtis, licensed to let Post-Horses." In 1813 it was still inhabited by a Curtis, but had ceased to be a posting-house. In 1861 the Misses Telford had the floors relaid, when a number of coins were found which had dropped between the boards. There were two silver sixpences of Queen Elizabeth, and coins of almost every reign since, also a quite fresh copper token of the White Hart, Bromley, dated 1660, a hart being engraved on one side. Besides these, several Roman Catholic, Latin, and English books, and some manuscript sermons, were discovered all concealed in the floors or wainscoting. Written inside of one of the books is a copy of verses, which convey a Roman Catholic or Protestant sentiment according as the lines are read from top to bottom, or from left to right. The verses are as follows:—

"I hold as faith
   What Rome's church saith
   Wheare the King's heade
   The flockes misleade
   Where the altares drest
   The people are blest
   He is but an asse
   That shunnes the masse
   What England's church allowes
   My conscience disallowes
   The church can have noe blame
   That houldes the Pope supreme
   The sacrifice is scarce divine
   With table bread and wine
   Who the communion flyes
   Is catholique and wise."

Rev. John Wesley, the celebrated divine of the eighteenth century, and the founder of the Wesleyan Methodist body, appears, from entries in his own journals, to have paid visits and preached at Widmore upon more than one occasion. He mentions the place by the name of Wigmore.

HAYES.

HAYES.

The origin of the name Hayes is to be found in the extensive heath or common-land, which to this day is one of the chief features of this pretty little country parish. In the middle of the sixteenth century the name was spelt Heese, and the place now known as Blackheath was then called Blakhese. Heese, = Heath, has gradually become altered to Hays, Haies, and finally, Hayes.

In walking from Bromley the traveller enters Hayes by way of Hayes Lane, and one of the first objects of interest he meets is the village inn—"The George"—which stands a little back from the village street, and is chiefly noticeable on account of its old painted signboard, illustrating the combat of St George and the Dragon. This painting is said to have been executed by Sir J. E. Millais, but whatever artistic merit it may formerly have displayed is now hidden by successive coats of varnish and exposure to the weather.

Hayes church spire, covered with oak shingles, which comes into sight at a turn in the road, looks modern; and a closer inspection shows that much of the body of the church is also modern; but upon entering the west door one may note, built into the wall, a few small fragments of carved stone of a distinctly Norman character. The Roman tiles built into the lower part of the tower also deserve attention. They are remnants, probably, of the Roman building which formerly stood upon the very ground which the church now occupies. The foundations of it were met with deep under ground when the north aisle was built. Two semi-circular headed windows still preserved in the walls of the church are certainly of Norman date, and lead to the belief that the Norman building which existed here was of an ecclesiastical nature. Of the Early English period an interesting relic was discovered when the south wall of the nave was pulled down to make room for the new south aisle. Fragments of an elegant triple lancet window, with moulded shafts of unornamented but shapely character, were found built into the wall. Upon the underside of a base was this inscription rudely cut, "P. D., 1599." The date may perhaps mark the year of the window's destruction, but whether the letters P. D. have any reference to the name of the destroyer it is hard to say. The modern triple niche over the west door of the church is of similar character to the fragments. It may be a reproduction of an earlier niche, the place of which it now occupies. Within the porch on the north and south sides are arches now filled up. South of the tower in the church's west wall is an interesting lancet—interesting as a relic of the old Early English Church, and as showing the thickness of the wall at this point. In the south-west corner of the south aisle is another interesting object. This is a quoin-stone, scored like a sun-dial, for which it was formerly used. By its guidance the bells were no doubt rung, and the time of the services of the church regulated. Its original place was at the south-west corner of the nave, and it was removed from that point only as far as necessary when the south aisle was added.

The chancel was lengthened and the north aisle added about the middle of the present century. The most recent addition—that of the south aisle and organ transept—is one which adds considerably to the beauty and uniformity of the Church. A brass plate within the church records the fact that the seats are to be free and unappropriated for ever. The benefactor's name is hidden under the modest designation of "a parishioner."

Hasted, writing of the church in his History of Kent (1778). says, "It consists of one ile and a chancel, and has a tower, on which is a low and rather unsightly pyramid; in it hang three bells." Since that description of the church appeared, many alterations have been effected. The church no longer consists of "one ile," but of three; the "rather unsightly pyramid" has been replaced by an elegant shingled spire; the three old bells remain, but three additional bells have been added. The following are their inscriptions:

1st bell. "Mears & Stainbank Founders London 1882."
2nd bell. "Mears & Stainbank Founders London 1882."
3rd. bell. "Mears & Stainbank Founders London 1882."
4th bell. "T Mears of London Fecit 1832."
5th bell. "John ✦ Hodson ✦ Made ✦ Me. 1670. C H."
6th bell. "Robertus Mot + Me fecit + 1602."

It is interesting to note that the ornamental cross upon the tenor bell, between the words "Mot" and "Me," was apparently made by an old stamp which had come into the possession of the founder. The same device has been noticed upon a fifteenth century bell at Little Halden, Herts.

Robert Mot appears to have been the first owner, as far as is known, of the Whitechapel Foundry. It is probable that he was a native of East Kent, and the son of one John Mott, of Canterbury, who was very busy in 1553 buying up hand-bells, organ pipes, latten candlesticks, and other loot from churches.*

* *Archæologia Cantiana*, xiv., p. 316 et seq.

BRASSES.

Of the monumental remains at Hayes Church the earliest now existing is the lid of a coped stone coffin, ornamented with a cross in relief, but much mutilated. This may belong to the 12th Century. It had been profanely used as a sill for the priest-door before the recent alteration of the church.

Upon the chancel floor are five small brasses all in memory of former rectors. The first in chronological order is that to John Osteler, who was rector of Hayes, according to Hasted's list of rectors, after the year 1488, but the exact date of his incumbency is not given by that authority, neither does the inscription enlighten us upon that point. Judging from the character of the brass, however, one would feel inclined to ascribe it to about the middle rather than to the end of the 15th Century. A demi-figure in brass, seven inches in length, represents John Osteler attired in eucharistic vestments, viz., amice (ornamented), albe, chasuble, and maniple. The hair, cropped above the ears, is wavy; the crown is shaven; and the hands, which are slender and delicate, are placed upon the breast in an attitude of devotion. Immediately under this is the following abbreviated latin inscription:

> Hic iacet dūs Johēs Osteler quōdam.
> Rector isti' ecclē cui' aīe ppiciet de'amen.

John Osteler appears to have been succeeded as rector by John Andrew,* but it does not appear whether the succession was immediate. The brass to his memory is inscribed with this quaint rhyme:

> I beseche you all that pasith here by for the
> Sowle of Sir John Andrew that here
> doth lye sey apater noster and an ave.

---

* The Osteler and Andrew brasses are dated approximately 1460 and 1470 in Murray's "Handbook."

Above the inscription is a figure in brass representing a full-length priest, 13½ inches in length, clad in eucharistic garb, viz., amice, albe with elegant apparels, stole, chasuble, and maniple. The feet are large and clumsy; the hands are placed naturally upon the breast; and the hair is dressed in the same manner as that of Osteler's effigy.

Another brass dated 1523, commemorating John Heygge, probably the next Rector of Hayes, has this inscription:

> Pray for yͤ soule of Sʳ John Heygge
> late pson of this church which decessid
> yͤ xix day of decēr Aº xvᶜ xxiii who' soul ihu pdn.

The brass to John Heygge possesses little artistic merit, but one or two points in which it differs from the earlier effigies deserve notice. The chasuble is proportionately larger, and is ornamented at the margin; the amice is smaller and apparently of a thinner material; the sleeves of the albe are larger; the stole and maniple have no terminal fringe; the hands are awkward, and the hair is nearly straight.

The fourth brass commemorates Robert Garret in the following inscription on a simple brass plate.*

> Hac cubant in fossa subpede Roberti Gar
> reti p'bri ossa, Rectoris olim ecclesiarum
> de Heys et Chesylhurst, Qui obiit . . . .
> die . . . . . . Anº dm̄ MᵒCCCCCᵒ lx . . .
> ppicius sit de' aie, R + Ga. Notarii publici.

The blank spaces for the date of death indicate that the brass was engraved during Garret's life. From an entry in the parish register it appears that he was buried on the 8th of May, 1566.

* In Thorpe's time, about 1770, this brass was fixed in the *wall* under the east window of the Chancel.

The fifth brass is that to the memory of John Hoare, bearing the following curious inscription:

> Who faine would lyve he must not feare to dye death is the waie
> That leades to lief and glorious Joies that tryumphes over Claie
> Come poore bewaile this want, Come ffriende lament & saie with me
> This man did dye to lyve, and lyves though dead his body be
> ffull xviii yeeres a Rector here he was, and then John Hoare
> unwedd deceast one thousand yeeres ffyve hundred [eightie fower]
>   the xi daie of ffebruarie
>   when he had lyvd lx score & three.

The sixth line is imperfect owing to the brass having been broken off, but the words "eightie fower" are supplied from Thorpe's transcript in his *Registrum Roffense*. The last line of the inscription is very odd. It should be thus read: $60 + 20 + 3 = 83$.

There is a line in Lysons' *Environs of London* which shows that an effigy formerly belonged to the brass. It seems to have disappeared many years ago, and it has been said that it was stolen by some workmen when the church was undergoing repair. If so perhaps the brass is still somewhere in the neighbourhood. Captain Edward Hoare (a descendant of Rev. John Hoare) on March 3rd, 1881, read a paper on the brasses in Hayes Church before a meeting of the Archæological Institute of Great Britain and Ireland, in which he spoke of the inscription on the Hoare brass as being unpublished. He was not aware apparently that it, together with all the other inscriptions on brass in Hayes Church, had been published by Dr John Thorpe in his *Registrum Roffense* more than a hundred years before.

A sixth brass is inserted in the floor of the north aisle. It bears this inscription:

HERE LYETH BVRYED IOHN HANDFORDE
THE SONNE OF HVMFREY HANDFORDE
OF LONDON MERCHAVNT BEINGE
EIGHT YEARES OLDE AND DIED THE
xvii[th] OF APRILL 1610.

MONUMENTS.

There is an interesting series of ledger stones in the north aisle chiefly in commemoration of members of the Scott Family, a branch of the Scotts, of Halden, in Kent, who were for many years seated at Hayes Place. When the alterations of the church necessitated a removal of these memorials, they were judiciously placed together at the east end of the aisle, where they may be inspected with convenience. The following are full transcripts of the inscriptions:—

On a blue ledger-stone, with the arms of
SCOTT, HACKET, and BROGRAVE.

Here resteth the body of S[r] Stephen Scott K[t] one of the Sonns of John Scott of Halden in the County of Kent Esq. he was a Gentleman pentioner to the late King Charles and was High Sherife of Kent in the yeare 1648. He maried Jane Morrall widow daughter to S[r] Cutbert Hacket K[t] His second wife was Elizabeth Brograve one of y[e] daughters of John Brograve Esq, by whom he had by Gods blessing 5 sonns & 4 daughters. After a long residence in this parish he removed his seate unto Chesthunt in Hartfordsheire where he departed this life in a good old age the 5th of June 1658 being 79 yeares and 10 months in hope of a Joyful Resurrection.

On a blue ledger-stone.

Nere this place lyeth buried Edmund Scott eldest Sonne of S. Stephen Scott who was borne ye 3 of August 1626 & died at 7 weekes ould and allso Stephen Scott 3 son of Sr Stephen Scott who die^d *——— of March 1633.

On a blue ledger-stone.

Here lyes buried underneath this stone John Scott Esq ye eldest sonn & heire of Sr Stephen Scott K^t of this County who married Dame Hester Style Widdow ye Relict of Sr Humphry Style of Langly K^t & Bar^t. He was one of his Maties Gent of his most hono^{ble} privy Chamber in ordinary & one of his Maties Justisses of ye peace in Corum for this County. He dyed ye 8 day of Aprill in ye yeare of our Lord 1670 and in ye 45 yeare of his age.

* "the 24th March, 1633." Thorpe's *Registrum Roffense*

On a blue ledger-stone, with the arms of
BRADGATE *and* SCOTT.

Heere lyeth the body of Elizabeth
the wife of Thomas Bradgate Mar
chant and eldest daughter of S. Step
hen Scott Kn. & Dame Elizabeth his
wife aged 26 yeares Shee dyed the
25 day o[f Sep]temb 1655. Shee left
issue [on]e sonn Martin and
one daughter Elizabeth.

On a blue ledger-stone, with the arms of
SCOTT.

Hic iacet sepultum corpus Annæ unius
filiarum Steph . . ni Scott Militis nuper
de hac parochia defuncti & uxoris
Gulielm Reeve de Fayrle in Insula
vectis, generosi quæ Obiit quinto
die Januarii Anno Salutis 1661
Ætatis Suæ xxxi°
Vita bona paucos numerat dies bonū
autem nomen permanebit in ævum.

On a grey ledger-stone.

He[re lyet]h intered ye body
of Ann Scott Daughter to
Stephen Scott Esq and
            Elizabeth his Wife
A younger Sonne to Sir
Stephen Scott of Hayes
deceased in her minoritie
being but six weekes old.

NOTE: Thorpe has preserved for us in his *Registrum Roffense* a fragment of another monumental inscription to the family of Scott, as follows:—

"On a grave stone are the following arms and inscription, viz. Two coats quarterly; 1st and 4th, a cross croslet; 2nd and 3rd, a chevron between three fleurs-de-lis.

> Here lyeth buried the worthie gentleman Sir Edmund Scott, knight, who was a v———r in anno 1597."

On a blue ledger-stone.

> Here lieth the Body of
> Mr. John Walwyn
> Mariner Son of a Worthy
> Clergy Man in Kent & Own
> Brother To ye Present Rector
> of this Church He died y^e
> 21st of May 1738. Over whose
> ashes His Relict
> Mrs Hannah Walwyn
> has placed this Monument
> of her Gratitude to his
> Memory. Aged 54 years.

The following is a list of the mural tablets and monuments within the church:—

South Aisle. Marble Tablet.
    Rev. John Till, for 50 years Rector of this Parish, died 13th February 1827.

South Aisle. Marble Tablet.
    William Joseph Coltman, Esq., died July 18th, 1818.

South Aisle. Marble Tablet.
    Ann Yarwood, died 20 April, 1736.
    Charles Yarwood, died 4 Jany., 1741.

South Aisle. Marble Tablet.
    John Hinton, died May 11th, 1781.
    Sarah, his widow, afterwards the wife of S. A. Cumberlege, died 10 Novr 1784.

West Wall of Nave.   Marble Tablet.

    Sir Vicary Gibbs Knt., one of His Majesties most
    honourable Privy Council, died Feb. 8th, 1820
    "He lived, and died, a firm friend to the Constitution
    of this Country both in Church and State."

North Aisle.   Mural Brass.

    Lieut John Arthur Smith, 47th Regiment, died 13 April 1875.

North Aisle.   Mural Brass.

    William Whateley, M.A., died 15th Novr. 1862.
    Elizabeth Martha his wife, died 14th February, 1868.

North Aisle.   Marble Tablet.

    Ann wife of Wm. Cleaver, died 5 May 1737.
    William Fenton, Esq., buried July 22, 1753.
    Jane, daughter of William and Ann Cleaver, and
    wife of William Fenton, died 21 May 1782.

North Aisle.   Mural Brass.

    Williamina Barbara Traill, died August 9th, 1862.
    James Traill, died October 16th, 1873.
    Caroline Traill, died July 10th, 1858.
    Janet Sinclair Traill, died January 17th, 1857.
    Janet Mary Traill, died September 1st, 1883.
    George Multon Traill, died May 31st, 1870.

Parish Church Goods.

One of the effects of the Reformation was to render useless nearly all of the costly and elaborate ecclesiastical vestments and furniture which had formed an important part in the services of the Roman Catholic Church. In the year 1552, Edward VI., in consequence of information that some of such church goods had been embezzled, or removed, contrary to his express commands, issued a commission to enquire into the whole matter, and to make a return in writing to the King's Council. It was ordered that as many of the old vestments or utensils as were necessary to the due and proper performance of the reformed services should be preserved to the use of the church, " leaving . . in every Parish Church or Chappell of common resort, one, two, or more Chalices or Cups, according to the multitude of the People in every such Church or Chappell, and also such other Ornaments as by their discretion shall seem requisite for the Divine Service in every such place for the time." ("The Church-History of Britain, endeavoured by Thomas Fuller" 1655, fol. Book vii., Sec. 2, p. 418.) The Record Office possesses an interesting collection of these inventories, and among them is the list relating to the church goods at Hayes, which is here given in full, as transcribed in *Archæologia Cantiana*, vol. ix., pp. 268-9.

"[Hayes] Heese—xxiii November vi. Ed. VI.
William Dryland, parson; William Frenche, &
Edward Kechell, churchwardens.

First ii chalics with their patents of silver whereof on of them with his patent all gilte weying x ouncs, thother viii ouncs.
Item iii bells suted & one saints bell
Item ii old copes thone grene silke thother blewe silke
Item a vestment of red silke imbrothered with birds & starrs
Item an old vestment of tynsell satten
Item an old vestment of blacke satten of bridgs*
Item an old vestment of blacke Russells worsted
Item an old vestment of blewe single sarcenet
Item v albes, v amysses

* Satin of Bruges.

Item v corporaxes* with theire cases
Item ii crosse clothes thone grene silke thother red silke
Item ix banner clothes of lynnen cloth painted
Item a surples & a rochet of lynnen cloth
Item a fonte cloth of lynnen
Item ii old diaper towells
Item iii font clothes on tawnye silke & other ii of lynnen cloth
Item a pix of latten, & an ewer of brasse
Item a bible & the paraphrases.

Mem. endorsed Dertford xxiii November vi. Ed. vi. All goods in the inventory of iii Ed vi are in this & are now delivered to the Churchwardens excepte ii curteynes presented to be stollen, and also except one chalice with the patent of silver weying vii ounces a hand-bell a sacryng bell ii litle bells a vaile clothe a clothe to hang before the roode iiii curteyns ii gret candlestikks of latten an old paire of organes, xiii latten candlestikks for tapers iii laten braunches iii crosses & a crosse staff, ii herse basens of latten a basen for the lampe a Crismatory of latten a basen for an ewer on holy water stopp & a paire of censers of latten lyke wyse presented to be sold for reparacions of the churche."

The term "paire of organes" means an organ of two stops. At Ashford, and Holy Cross, in Canterbury, there were "two pair of organs." An organ was worth, it is supposed, about £10; so the existence of one at Hayes previous to the year 1552, shows that the church was possessed of some amount of wealth as well as a taste for music and elaborate services.

* Vessels used for the reservation of the Eucharist for the sick. They were often covered by a thin veil of silk or muslin.

Parish Register.

The Parish Registers of Hayes date from the year 1539. The earliest entries are contained in a curious long vellum book, bearing upon its first page the following title:

A true Regis

ter Booke for the parishe of Hays in the Countye of Kente: of All the Names and Surnames of all suche persons As have beene Baptyzed Married and Buryed in the saide parishe of Hays synce the Yeare of our Lorde God One thousand five hundred thirtye and Nine And the one and thirtyes Yeare of the Raigne of the most famous Kynge of Noble Memory Kynge **Henrie** the Eighte:

Extracts from Hayes Parish Register, with notes.

"Robert Davidson Mr: of Arts & Minr: of Down was instituted Rector of Hayes December ye 15th, & inducted into the parish-Church there on the 17th of the said month Anno Dom. 1696, Having been presented thereunto by Robert Uvedale Dr. of Lawes & Rector of Orpington; Dr Thomas Tenison being Ld. archbp. of Canterbury."

"The Revnd. Mr. Robert Davidson late Rect. of Hayes was Buried May ye 27 1714, and lies on the North side of ye Comunion Table within the Rails."

Mr Davidson was the author of a Sermon on the Thanksgiving Day (1st May 1707), for the successful union of the Parliaments of England and Scotland. The title of the Sermon is:—

"*Brit.* ANN. ia.
A
Sermon
Preach'd on the
Thanksgiving-Day.
for the
Happy Union
of
Great Britain.
Under Her Sacred Majesty Queen
Anne, *May* the 1*st*, 1707.
By Robert Davidson, Rector
Of *Hayes* in *Kent*.
London:
Printed by *R. Tookey* for the Author. MDCCVII." *

"James Bruce Esqr of Lincolns Inn & Adriana Allen of All-Hallows Staining of London was Married February the 8: 1754."

James Bruce is said to have been descended from the royal house of Bruce, but it is in the character of a traveller that he is best known. Born at Kinnaird, Stirlingshire, 1730, and educated at Harrow and Edinburgh, he came to London and entered into partnership with a wine-merchant, whose daughter, Adriana Allen, he married. In 1762 he was appointed Consul-General in Algiers, and in 1765 he commenced his travels in Northern Africa and Asia Minor. Three years later he departed on his tour to explore

* A copy of this tract is preserved in the Library of King George III., at the British Museum.

the source of the Nile. He returned to England in 1773, and in 1790 he published his celebrated "Travels to discover the Source of the Nile," a book which contains much curious information, has gone through numerous editions, and has been translated into French and German.

"John son of the Honourable William and Lady Esther Pitt was born the 10th of October and baptized the 7th Novr 1756."

Viscount Pitt succeeded as 2nd Earl of Chatham, 11 May, 1778.

"William son of the Rt Honble William and Lady Esther Pitt was born the 28th of May and baptized the third day of July 1759."

William Pitt the celebrated Statesman and Prime Minister, spent much of his early life at Hayes. Sometimes birdsnesting in the neighbouring woods, and always taking a deep interest in the occupations of the servants at Hayes Place, he seems to have enjoyed a happy and homely boyhood. When he became older he developed a strong liking for planting trees. He would work early in the morning and late at night to accomplish his projected schemes of planting. The fine and rare trees in the grounds of Holwood have with very good reason been attributed to his selection. When Prime Minister, he superintended the planting of Baston, at that time the property of a Mr Randall, a merchant. Mr Randall, owing to the pressure of business matters, was unable to conduct the planting himself, but Mr Pitt found time for it during his journeys from Holwood (where he then lived) to Westminster.

Dr Anthony Addington, a local medical practitioner, attended Mr Pitt in a severe illness, and succeeded in restoring him to health by a course of treatment which included the seductive remedy of port wine. Dr Addington's son, Henry, afterwards Viscount Sidmouth, was intimate with William Pitt from childhood, and this intimacy seems to have led him to adopt a political career. In 1783 he was elected M.P. for Devizes, and in 1789 he became Speaker of the House of Commons, mainly, as it is supposed, through the influence of his friend Mr Pitt.

The great Earl of Chatham (Pitt's father) lived at Hayes Place for several years, and might often be seen riding about Hayes Common. A bridle-path in the enclosed part of the common, leading from Coney Hall Farm towards Baston, is still known as Lord Chatham's Walk. He was seized with a fit suddenly in the House of Lords on the 8th of April 1778, and removed to his seat at Hayes Place, where he expired on the 11th May following. A public funeral and a noble monument in Westminster Abbey were voted by Parliament, and a pension of £4000 a year was settled on his heirs in perpetuity. The banners used at Lord Chatham's funeral were formerly kept in the chancel of Hayes Church, but they became dilapidated and were removed many years ago, although they have been frequently referred to as still existing in the Church in modern books with a persistency which shows how little trouble the writers have taken to verify the correctness of their assertions (see Murray's "Handbook," 1877 ed., and Loftie's "Round about London," 1880 ed., &c.).

"19 Dec. 1774 Charles Lord Viscount Mahon of the Parish of Chevening in the County of Kent Batchelor and the Right Hon[ble] Lady Hester Pitt of this Parish Spinster were Married in this Parish by Special License at the Earl of Chatham's this nineteenth day of December in the Year One Thousand seven Hundred and seventy four by me E. Wilson, Chaplain to the Earl of Chatham."

The celebrated and erratic Lady Hester Lucy Stanhope was a daughter of that marriage.

"Francis Fawkes M.A. was instituted April 1774 to the Rectory of Hayes in Kent void by the decease of the Revd William Farquhar; being presented thereto by the Rev^d Dr Charles Plumptre Rector of Orpington. Died August 26, 1777."

Rev. Francis Fawkes was a divine and poet of some eminence. He translated the works of Anacreon, Sappho, Bion, Moschus, Musæus, Theocritus, and Apollonius Rhodius. He published in 1761 an edition of the Holy Scriptures, with notes, called "The Complete Family Bible." He was also the author of "Original Poems and Translations," 1761, and "Partridge-Shooting; an eclogue," 1767, and also, in conjunction with William Woty, he edited "The Poetical Calendar," 1763.

"John Till L.L.B. was instituted October 4th & inducted October 7th 1777 to the Rectory of Hayes in Kent void by the decease of the Revd Francis Fawkes; being presented thereto by the Rev^d Dr Charles Plumptre, Rector of Orpington."

Mr Till, Rector of Hayes for nearly fifty years, was a man much beloved by his parishioners, and his memory is still cherished with deep respect and affection. To an amiable disposition he added a considerable share of pleasantry and dry humour. The following impromptu toasts which he gave at the village school-feasts, in which he much delighted, are worth preserving.

> "May our School be the friend of the Church and the Crown:
> May it often break up;—May it never break down."

> "May virtue and learning still thrive in our School,
> And our duty to God and the King be our rule.
> May we keep to this rule to the end of our days,
> And always remember we learnt it at Hayes."

> "May our School be kept up by the wise and discerning,
> And always be famed for plum-pudding and learning."

Mr Till's entries in the Parish Registers are characterised by great care and precision, and he has copied out in fair handwriting some of the old entries which were badly written.

"John Mumford of Hayes, aged 98 years was buried September 27th, 1839, by Sir Charles Farnaby, Officiating Minister."

John Mumford was for many years a servant in Lord Chatham's household. His memories of Lord Chatham, Mr Pitt, and Admiral Byng were most interesting. When Admiral Byng was shot at Portsmouth on March 14th, 1757, it was his servant John Mumford who arranged the cushion upon which the Admiral knelt. An interesting account of John Mumford, taken from the "Mirror," appeared in the *Bromley Record* of September 1860.

Hayes Place.

The house in which the great Earl of Chatham died, and in which the celebrated William Pitt, his second son, was born, cannot fail to possess strong claims upon the interest of every Englishman, and, for that reason, we shall devote a few lines to a description of this place, which was the scene of both those events, and is rich with other historical associations. The house is situated near Hayes Church, but is partly hid from view by trees and a brick wall which skirts the road. It is a plain square mansion of comfortable and roomy proportions. The estate was once the property of a branch of the family of Scott, of Halden, in Kent, and it was alienated by Stephen Scott, Esq., to Mr John Harrison of Southwark. Several members of the Scott family lie buried in Hayes Church, and their monumental inscriptions may be seen there upon the floor of the north aisle. Mr

Harrison sold Hayes Place, in 1754, to the Right Hon. William Pitt, afterwards the first Earl of Chatham. In 1756 John, afterwards the second Earl, was born here, and on the 28th of May 1759 William Pitt, the younger, was born. The room in which that illustrious statesman first saw the light is situated upon the ground floor, and is now used as a schoolroom. The event is duly entered in the Parish Register of Hayes.

Of William Pitt's early days at Hayes there is nothing left to remind us. There are no portraits or relics now existing there; but, until quite recently, there was an old wooden step for mounting a horse—*jossing-block* is the local name—which was interesting as having served as a platform from which the younger Pitt, when a small boy, at his father's desire, made speeches to an imaginary audience. It is much to be regretted that this interesting relic was recently destroyed by some of the servants of the household who were ignorant of its history. It has been said that William Pitt, when a boy, used to go birdnesting in the woods at Holwood, and his desire to possess that seat for his own, as he told Lord Bathurst, dated from those early days. Pitt's ambition was gratified. In the autumn of 1785 he purchased Holwood.

Soon after the purchase of Hayes Place by the elder Pitt, considerable sums of money were expended upon its improvement. The house, as he bought it, was a square building of red brick. To this he made the addition of a square building on the south side of the main block. The two buildings are connected by a covered passage. Other important and expensive improvements were made. To the north of Hayes Place, and divided from it by an old road, there was a small estate and house. Mr Pitt diverted the road, purchased the estate, pulled down the house, and added the land to his own. The old road, of which some indications exist in the grounds, originally ran along the north side of Hayes Place. When it was diverted, the present road past "Jacob's Well" was constructed. The plantations of Hayes Place are generally thought to have been directed by Pitt; and this is probable, because they seem to have been planned with a view of securing the privacy of the house and grounds—an object in entire harmony with Pitt's peculiar mental condition. "The truth is," says Lord Macaulay, "that he had for some time been in an unnatural state of excitement. No suspicion of this sort had yet got abroad. His eloquence had never shone with more splendour than during the recent debates. But people afterwards called to mind many things which ought to have roused their apprehensions. His habits were gradually becoming more and more eccentric. A horror of all loud sounds, such as is said to have been one of the many oddities of Wallenstein, grew upon him. Though the most affectionate of fathers, he could not at this time bear to hear the voices of his own children, and laid out great sums at Hayes in buying up houses contiguous to his own, merely that he might have no neighbours to disturb him with their noise." In 1766 Mr Pitt was advanced to the titles of Viscount Pitt of Burton Pynsent, in Somersetshire, and Earl of Chatham, in Kent. Among other distinguished people who visited Hayes Place may be mentioned General Wolfe, the Duke of Cumberland, and the Prince of Brunswick. Earl Chatham sold Hayes Place in 1766 to the Hon. Thomas Walpole, but so fond was he of the estate that he bought it back again in the next year.

The scene of Lord Chatham's fall in the House of Lords has been portrayed by a master-hand in Copley's celebrated picture, which now hangs in the National Gallery. The picture is generally spoken of as depicting the death of Chatham, but this is not quite accurate, as Lord Chatham did not die in the House of Lords. He fell in a fit on the 8th of April 1778. As soon as possible he was removed to Hayes Place, his favourite residence. There he languished until the 11th of May following, when he died. The room in which he passed away is on the first floor in the north angle of the house, and is still used as a bedroom. One of its windows is shown on the right hand side of the engraving of Hayes Place, which is here given.

HAYES PLACE.

After Lord Chatham's death Hayes Place was retained by his family only for a few years, and in 1785 was by them alienated to James Bond, Esq. From the latter it passed to the Right Hon. George Viscount Lewisham, eldest son of the Earl of Dartmouth. Finally it has passed into the hands of Everard A. Hambro, Esq., who now owns the estate. To Mr Hambro my best thanks are due for personally showing me round his most interesting and historic house.

Pickhurst Manor.

This manor, formerly known as Heaver, lies in that part of Hayes parish which borders upon Beckenham. In 1693 it was the property of Matthias Wallraven, Esq., whose grandson Peter in 1757 alienated it to William Cowley, Esq., and he sold it in 1765 to Mariabella Eliot. In 1798 the place was the property of J. Eliot, Esq., and the residence of John Bowdler, Esq. In 1830 Lady Hawarden lived there. Since then it has been successively rented by Lady Caroline Morland, Colonel Cator (now Sir John Lennard, Bart.), Lord Kinnaird, and C. F. Devas, Esq., J.P. It is the property of Mrs Howard, the widow of a descendant of J. Eliot, Esq.

Tye-Pig (? Tithe Pig) is the name of a cottage close by.

Pickhurst may have been formerly Pighurst, *i.e.*, Pigwood, or land for the pannage of hogs, for which purpose the abundance of acorns which one finds there would render it specially suitable.

Baston Manor.

Baston Manor House, the residence of Captain Torrens, is pleasantly situated on the edge of Hayes Common, and commands varied and extensive views on all sides. Externally the house presents no feature of antiquarian interest, but about the year 1813 Mr Alfred John Kempe was so fortunate as to discover in one of the rooms a series of most interesting and curious painted oak panels of the latter part of the fifteenth century. Mr Kempe in the *Gentleman's Magazine* of December 1830 gave an interesting account, with engravings, of these ancient paintings. From that account the following details are taken. The panels had been used to form the wainscot of a small closet, and, in order to fit the vacant spaces of the wall, they had been barbarously mutilated by the saw, and arranged without reference to the subjects of the pictures, so that some of the figures were standing upon their heads instead of their feet. A paper-hanger and stencil-painter from London, employed in the house, was requested to devote some of his talent and taste to the beautifying of the old paintings, " supplying them with new beards and noses, as he might think necessary, renovating the lustre of their eyes, or accommodating them with new ones if the old should appear beyond repair." Mr Kempe fortunately rescued the paintings from that fate. Two sound panels nearly six feet in height, each bearing a representation of a regal figure, escaped almost unscathed. One of the royal personages seated under a cloth of estate, his rich crimson robe powdered with golden *A's*, is a representation of the Saxon King Athelstan. The back ground to this figure is formed by a delineation of tapestry, in which is worked a shield charged with a cross patée. King Athelstan occupies a stone or marble bench. His hair is depicted of an auburn colour. A sceptre formed of three golden rods is held in the left hand, and a globe in the right. At the feet of the figure was an inscription, of which the following was legible:

> Athelstanus Edwardi . . . filius . . . regnavit anno . . . . . d . . . . et consecravit sanctus . . . . tanus hic reges Wallensium et Scot . . . . pacem recepit eos sub se regnare . . . . .

An attempted translation is as follows:

Athelstane, the son of Edward the elder, reigned fifteen years; holy Wulfstan consecrated him. He conquered the Kings of Wales and Scotland, received them to his peace, and suffered them to govern under him.

The other paintings bear no inscription, and the persons represented are subjects of conjecture. The erect regal figure, with crown and sceptre in right hand, has been supposed to represent Edward IV. Mr Kempe, as a mere surmise, suggested that it might represent Constantine, King of Scots. Another panel, less perfect than the two just mentioned, bears the representation of a youthful figure in the attitude of prayer, and crowned as a prince. A square fragment of another panel bears a head with a singularly-formed red cap, lined with blue, and topped by a round button.

Judging from the costumes of the figures, &c., the date of the paintings has been fixed with some amount of certainty at about 1480. Mr Stodard informed Mr Kempe that they were the earliest paintings in oil which he had ever seen.* The colouring is exceedingly rich and deep, and has been well contrasted by the use of a pigment of real gold in the crowns, sceptres, borders of garments, &c. It is satisfactory to know that these interesting relics are out of the reach of vandalism. They are now preserved in the rooms of the Society of Antiquaries of London, where they hang in the hall, near the stairs leading to the Library, belonging to that body.

* The use of oil paints was known in the ninth century.

Pit Dwellings at Hayes Common.

The existence of ancient earthworks at Hayes Common was, as far as I have been able to ascertain, first publicly adverted to in the year 1878, when Mr Flinders Petrie read a paper on "Kentish Earthworks" before the Kent Archæological Society at Bromley. In that paper they were referred to briefly as "enclosures, entrenchments, pit-villages, and tumuli," and as "the finest in Kent for their extent, their preservation, and the great number of pit-dwellings, exceeding one hundred and fifty." The existence of such remains had, however, been noticed and pointed out some years before that date by the late Rector of Hayes, Rev. G. V. Reed. It does not appear that any steps were taken towards excavating or closely examining the remains until December 1878, when the writer dug out one of the supposed pit-dwellings, but with no satisfactory result. The digging revealed the presence of disturbed earth of a depth of about eighteen inches. In the following summer (August 1879) I opened two or three other pits with a similarly unsuccessful result. But in one very small pit, about four feet in diameter, near Baston Manor, I was fortunate in finding distinct indications of an ancient fire buried under a deposit of earth upwards of a foot in thickness. The disturbed earth consisted of five distinct strata, of which the following is a list:—

No. 1. Turf and surface peat,   5 inches deep.
,, 2. Black earth, with charcoal, . . $1\frac{1}{2}$,,
,, 3. White sand, with reddened pebbles, $2\frac{1}{2}$,,

No. 4. Black earth, with fine charcoal, . 4 inches deep.
„ 5. Black earth, containing large pieces of charcoal, fine charcoal, reddened pebbles, &c., . . 5 „

Total depths to undisturbed earth, 18 inches.

NOTE.—Below this the pebble-beds had not been disturbed, but the fire, of which such evident indications remained in the bed of black earth (No. 5), had coloured the pebbles considerably. One or two pebbles *in situ* had acquired a reddish tinge upon their upper surface only, proving that this was the bottom of the fire, and probably the floor upon which it was kindled. The reddened pebbles in stratum No. 3 had probably been used as pot-boilers.

In 1886 I made further excavations at Hayes Common, by means of which several important facts were brought to light. Selecting a pit, near the eastern limits of the Common, of remarkable and promising appearance, on the 16th of September I commenced by digging a deep trench through it from east to west. The pit consisted of a large depression, nearly circular, 17 feet in diameter, raised conical mound in the centre, and the unusual feature of a square addition upon the eastern side. Whether the latter should be considered the foundation of a separate apartment or that of a porch to screen the entrance from the east wind does not appear. It is a curious fact, however, that in some of the beehive huts in Cornwall a somewhat similar arrangement may be found. At Zennor there are several such huts, consisting of a circular apartment with two entrances, and a square apartment attached, access to which from the circular room is gained by a low doorway. It may be remarked that for a living-room a circular form would be the best adapted, just as for a sleeping-room a square-shaped apartment would be the most convenient and best suited to the recumbent body. Such an explanation as this seems to fit in very well this curious arrangement of chambers, although the evidences are not sufficiently clear to allow one to speak positively upon the matter. At a depth of 26 inches from the top of the central mound, the hard, undisturbed soil was encountered. Just before reaching that depth about thirty large pebbles were turned up by the spade. The depth at which they were found must have been from 21 to 22 inches. Some of the largest pebbles were 6 inches in greatest length. Possibly these pebbles may have served as a hearth in the centre of the living-room, but, if so, there could have been but little fire as they are not much coloured by fire.

On September 23rd I dug trenches through two small pits situated nearly in the middle of Hayes Common. The first pit was a small circular depression 8 feet 6 inches in diameter. At a depth of 7 inches from the surface I found a small flint flake in a bed of sand. Neither the flint nor the clayey sand in which it was embedded bore any marks of fire, but, just below, at a depth of 8 inches from the surface, the hard, undisturbed earth was encountered. The marks of fire were very decided. The pebbles had been reddened, and in some cases burnt to a white condition, and the sandy loam in which they lay had become hardened and partially baked by the extreme heat to which it had been subjected. The flake bore no mark of fire, therefore it was probably deposited where I found it after the time of the fire below it.

Another pit close by, 8 feet 6 inches in diameter, also showed marks of severe fire-action.

It has been computed that the total number of so called "pit-dwellings" at Hayes Common is about 150. After a careful examination of every specimen I have come to the conclusion that they are capable of being divided into three types, viz. :—

1. Large circular pits, from 10 to 20, or even 30 feet in diameter, and from 6 inches to 2 feet 6 inches deep, surrounded by a well-defined and carefully constructed mound, in which, at one point, there is a flat space—probably the old entrance to the hut. They contain no considerable remains of fire.
2. Large circular pits, similar in every way to the above, but with a low conical mound in the centre.
3. Small circular pits, very even and uniform in construction, from 4 feet to 10 feet in diameter, without marks of entrance, and generally without any encircling mound, but always containing, at a depth of about a foot or less, reddened pebbles, charred wood, and other indications of fire. In some of them I have found fragments of oak wood thoroughly burnt to charcoal.

No ancient pottery at all was found, although the number of hut-floors uncovered was sufficiently large to reveal it had it been present in any quantity. About 20 or 30 flint implements, chiefly flakes and arrow points, have been found at Hayes Common. They are inferior in every way to those found by the writer at West Wickham.

Ancient Earthworks at Toots Wood.

Toots Wood is in the parish of Beckenham, bordering upon that of Hayes, but as some of the earthworks therein appear to be connected with earthworks in Hayes parish, it may be well to give some particulars of them here. I am indebted for the following information to Mr W. J. Nichols of Woodside, South Hill, Bromley, who has paid great attention to the subject, and knows every inch of the ground in and around Toots Wood. To the same gentleman I am indebted for drawing my attention to the ancient earthworks, and personally showing them to me.

Bromley was probably a place of some importance at an early age before the Roman occupation of the country. South Hill is situated about half a mile south of Bromley Church, and still retains a very picturesque piece of woodland, in which are some fine oak trees. This is Toots Wood, which, with its continuation, Kingswood, doubtless formed part of an ancient forest. Places named Tot Hill, Toot Hill, or Tooter Hill, are very numerous, and Rev. Isaac Taylor, in his "Words and Places," considers that they may possibly have been dedicated to the worship of the Celtic deity Taith.

The earthworks at Toots Wood are of a rather remarkable form. They are near the crown of the hill upon the north-western side, and consist of a series of six inverted conical pits, opening out to a diameter of considerable size—in one case, 100 ft. × 250 ft. The depth is about 20 feet, and the lowest portion of each pit is occupied by a small pool of water, and a large quantity of partially decayed vegetable matter. A very large quantity of earth must have been removed in the formation of these pits, and, as it does not appear to have been deposited around the sides of the excavations, Mr Nichols suggests that it may have been spread evenly over the higher part of the hill and upon its western slope, where a considerable depth of moved earth has been observed. The accumulation of water in the bottom of these pits is attributed to the construction of a new road which has cut off their original drainage.

In the summer of 1885 Mr Nichols caused a trench to be dug into the vegetable soil at the bottom of the largest pit, and at a depth of less than two feet from the surface about thirty or forty fragments of Roman and mediæval pottery were discovered. The fragments of Roman pottery are of a dark bluish-grey colour, and much like that known as Upchurch ware in general appearance, but of coarser texture. Among the fragments of pottery attributed to mediæval times are two or three large pieces which have been parts of a large, wide-mouthed jar, of a capacity perhaps of two gallons. There were also found at the same place fragments of partially-baked pottery, molar teeth of horse much blackened and hardened, burnt bone, wood of the character of bog-oak, and flint stones. There were considerable traces of iron, but the only piece obtainable in anything approaching form appears to be a spear-head. A mediæval silver coin and a sharp fragment of flint, possibly an arrow-head, were also found in the same pit.

Other pits similar to these have existed near Toots Wood Road, and parts of them still exist, but they have been modified or partially filled up by recent alterations. There are remains of another pit, now converted into two ponds, near Pickhurst Farm House.

The purpose of these remarkable excavations appears somewhat uncertain—the absence of defensive works being a serious objection to the theory, expressed by some, that they form portions of a British Camp. In the absence of any better explanation, I would suggest that their purpose was the same as that of the hiding-pits upon the Coombe Hills near Croydon, described by King in his *Munimenta Antiqua* (Vol. I., p. 50 *et seq.*), *i.e.*, the hiding of soldiers during military operations. The only objection to this theory is that the Toots Wood pits are in all cases more or less occupied by water, whereas those mentioned by King are remarkable for the fact that they always remain dry, even after heavy rain.

The great age of the pits at Toots Wood is shown by the timber trees now growing in them, apart from the Roman and other remains which Mr Nichols has been so fortunate as to find; and their occurrence at a place named after a Celtic deity suggests the question whether they may or may not have been connected with the worship of that deity. In the ancient road (which Toots Wood Road now follows) were found some remains of flint and septaria foundations about a foot below the surface, 2 feet broad, and about 6 or 7 feet in length, and about 1 foot in depth. Remains of foundations of the same kind and size were found about a hundred paces further towards Hayes Lane. Beneath one of the pieces of septaria was found a molar tooth of a deer. Mr Nichols enquires, "May not these remains have been associated with early British sports, or for the more serious purpose of sacrifice?"

Traces of an old road running parallel with Hayes Lane may be seen in Langley Park. Another ancient road leads from a point in Hayes Lane near Pickhurst Farm in the direction of Bromley, and extends for a distance of about a quarter of a mile. It has been hollowed out, and an earth wall raised on each side. Measured across, from the crest of each wall, it is 17 feet, and the depth from that line to the present bottom of the road is 2 feet 6 inches. A deposit of decayed vegetable matter and water now occupies this old covered road, which was no doubt deep enough originally to afford a secret and safe channel for passengers in times of disturbance or war.

Jacob's Well.

A spring of water by the roadside, near the ornamental ponds in the grounds of Hayes Place, is known locally as Jacob's Well. It has been enclosed in a sort of rude stone niche, and a hollowed stone has been placed as a basin to receive the water as it slowly flows from the bank of earth which skirts the road. The stone employed for the purpose appears to be a tough kind of limestone, and it contains numerous fossil remains. It is said that this work was done at the expense of Mr Jacob Angus, formerly of this parish, and that it was probably done at the beginning or early part of the present century.

KESTON.

KESTON.

The name Keston has been supposed by Hasted to have been derived from Chestan or from Chesterton, that is, the place of a camp or fortification. In three Anglo-Saxon charters the place called "Cystaninga Mearce" is mentioned as one of the boundaries of the land. This was undoubtedly some well known portion of boundary line or markland at Keston, the name of which is preserved to this day in the name Keston Mark, a public house at Keston near the boundary of the parish. Mr Corner, therefore, with good reason gives the following derivation: "This name of Cystaning seems to be composed of *cyst*, a chest or coffin; *stanc*, a stone; and *ing*, a field. It would thus mean 'The field of stone coffins,' a name singularly applicable to a spot where sepulchral remains, including stone coffins of a date anterior to the Anglo-Saxon name of the place, have been found."

Windmills.

There have been three windmills at Keston at various times. One was situated just above Wilberforce's Oak in Holwood Park, but no trace now remains of it, except a small space of level ground upon which it formerly stood. I have been unable to ascertain the exact date of its removal, but it is hardly likely that the mill stood at that spot after Mr Pitt made so large an addition to Holwood Park as he did in 1790, when he enclosed a large portion of Keston Common, including the site of the old windmill. The windmill which formerly stood near the Fox Inn, facing Hayes Common, was so much damaged by a severe gale of wind, that it had to be taken down several years ago. The third mill still stands on the western margin of Keston Common, and is a picturesque object in the landscape for many miles round. It is one of the old-fashioned post-mills, which are now becoming scarce in consequence of the introduction of steam power. Although it is past work, its owner, J. S. Gainsford, Esq., preserves it for the sake of its picturesque appearance. The date upon the present mill-post (a fine solid piece of timber, two feet square) is 1716, but there was an older mill upon the same site, which this mill replaces.

The Archdeacon's Well.

At a bend in the road between Keston Common and the Parish Church, just above War Bank, there still exists the Archdeacon's Well, made "for the Public Good, April, 1735," by Rev. Archdeacon Christopher Clarke, at that time Rector of the Parish of Keston. It is a square well about five feet deep, and constructed of brick, but now covered over by a flagstone. The spring is of pure water, and is abundant even in periods of long drought, when all the water sources are exhausted at Down, and the inhabitants of which place come hither to draw.

Cæsar's Well.

Cæsar's Well, the chief source of the Ravensbourne, is situated near the entrance gates to Holwood Park. Mr Hone's interesting "Table Book," written in the year 1828, contains an account of a visit paid, in company with his friend W—, to the source of the Ravensbourne. At the time of that visit it would appear that the spring was locally known as the " Bath." In the time of Mr Pitt's residence at Holwood it was much used as a bath, and its waters were supposed to be possessed of valuable medicinal properties. Hasted's plan of the camp at Holwood (pub. in 1778) shows the well or bath, and twelve trees are represented as growing close round its margin, and there are appearances of steps leading down to the water. The article in Hone's "Table-Book" to which reference has been made, is illustrated by an engraving, which shows the spring to be irregular in form and partially surrounded by rushes. The pond beyond is shown to be small and much further from the spring than is the present pond. The engraving shows also a fence in the distance, which, it is evident, occupied the same place as that one now does which runs along by the roadside between the middle and lowermost ponds. Since the time when that engraving was executed a considerable change has taken place. Two ponds have been made where formerly was but one, and the well has been repaired. The date of these works was probably about the year 1831 or 1832.

The name Ravensbourne is commonly supposed to take its origin from the following tradition. When the Roman soldiers were encamped at Holwood there was great need of water. A raven was seen to frequent a certain spot near the camp, and upon close examination a small spring was discovered among the bushes. Upon digging out the place a copious spring was found, and from the accident which led to that discovery it is supposed the stream took its name. Unfortunately for this theory the word raven is of Teutonic rather than Latin origin. There are indications of a path leading through the ramparts of the camp to the spring. The earthworks upon Keston Common, facing the National Schools, appear to have been constructed for the defence of the spring, which to a large army of soldiers, quartered in such a camp as that at Holwood, would be a matter of the first necessity, especially as there is no spring in the camp.

Holwood Camp.

Just above Cæsar's Well are some clear remains of a fine old British Camp. Its west and north sides stand out in commanding boldness; on the opposite side, alas! the levelling spade of the gardener has converted the ramparts into a lawn. The original shape of the work was oval, like so many other camps of pre-Roman origin, and the area enclosed within its lines of circumvallation has been computed at about twenty-nine acres. Towards the north-west and north there remain three distinct valla, and between the middle and the inmost valla is a ditch nearly twenty feet in depth, but in other parts there appear to have been only two valla, and they much lower. In the original work a palisade or *chevaux-de-frise* doubtless surmounted the ramparts, making anything like hostile invasion no easy undertaking. Probability is given to this view by the fact that when Mr Pitt destroyed part of the camp the workmen met with remains, embedded in the earth, of ancient and blackened trees, indicative of palisades. Holwood Camp, unlike Oldbury at Ightham and other British camps, has no spring of water within its circumference. The small pools which catch and for a time retain the rain, are dried up in the summer months. Hence the value of Cæsar's Well close by. A way out of the camp seems to have led down to the spring.

It has with good reason been pointed out that such works as these could not have been constructed by the advancing Romans so hastily as would have been necessary for their purpose. The ovoid shape, indicative of pre-Roman workmanship, and the magnitude of the work, both indicate that the Romans found Holwood Camp in existence when they established their power in this district. It is extremely probable that the Roman masters of Holwood improved the defensive strength of such a commanding and valuable military position.

"Some have imagined." says Hasted, " this was the camp which Julius Cæsar made when the Britons gave him the last battle with their united forces, just before he passed the Thames in pursuit of Cassivelaun;" but he adds, "its nearness to the Thames, its size, strength, and other circumstances, are inducements to think that it was the place where Aulus Plautius, the prætor, after his fourth action with the Britons, encamped with his forces whilst he waited the arrival of the Emperor Claudius." It may be added that several antiquaries agree with the learned Kentish topographer in this opinion.

Many sources have been suggested for the name Holwood, anciently Hollwood. Holly, holy, old, are amongst their number. but the most probable origin to my mind is one which seems hitherto to have been quite overlooked. Holt-wudu, the Anglo-

Saxon equivalent to the modern word wood or forest agrees remarkably well in sound to the modern name, and was, at the same time, quite characteristic of the spot to which it was applied.

A writer in the *European Magazine*, Vol. XXII., p. 416 (December 1792), thus refers to the camp:—

"This celebrated camp, till within these twenty years, was tolerably perfect; it consisted of a circular double, and in some places treble intrenchment, enclosing about twenty-nine acres of land; into which there appeared to have been no original entrance but by the opening to the north-west, which descends to the spring called Cæsar's spring. This spring has long been converted into a most useful public cold bath; a dressing house is built on the brink of it; it is ornamented with beautiful trees; and, from its romantic situation, forms a most pleasing scene.

"However antiquarians (from the variety of fragments, coins, &c., that have been discovered or ploughed up in the neighbourhood) may have been induced to differ in conjecture as to the person who framed it, they all agree this Camp to have been a strong and considerable Roman station, though not of the larger sort; but rather from its commanding situation, and short distance from the Thames, a Camp of Observation, or *Castra Æstiva*. At the same time there is great reason to suppose it to have been since possessed by other invaders."

An excellent plan of Holwood Camp was published 14th April 1806, in the *Vetusta Monumenta*, forming plate 10 of the fourth volume of that valuable work.

Holwood House.

In the year 1642 Sir Stephen Lennard was possessed of Holwood. It afterwards passed to Captain Pearch, "who settled it, in 1709, on the marriage of his niece, Elizabeth Whiflin, with Nathaniel Gatton, Esq., of Beckenham, in special tail. He left an only son and heir of the same name, whose only surviving daughter and heir, Mary Dippen, left Anne Dippen, her only surviving daughter and heir likewise; who in 1765 alienated this seat to Peter Burrell, Esq., of Beckenham, and he, in 1766, conveyed it to Wm. Ross, gent., of London, who in 1767 passed it away again to Robert Burrow, Esq., who made great improvements to it, and resided here till his death."—(Hasted's "History of Kent.") His eldest son, Christopher, left Robert Burrow the possessor of this seat, and he sold Holwood to a Mr Randall, a shipbuilder, from whom the estate was purchased in 1785 by the Right Hon. William Pitt. By an agreement with the vestry of Keston to pay £10 annually to the poor of the parish, Mr Pitt acquired the right to enclose a large piece of Keston Common, which he attached to Holwood Park. By judiciously cutting down trees and planting, the estate was still further improved and beautified. With what ardour Mr Pitt applied himself to planting will be seen in the following extract from a letter which he addressed from Downing Street to his mother on the 13th November 1786:—" To-morrow I hope to get to Holwood, where I am impatient to look at my works. I must carry there, however, only my passion for planting, and leave that of cutting entirely to Burton."

It is said that when night drew on the work of planting was not interrupted, but artificial light was brought, and the work was frequently completed by lantern light.

The quiet seclusion of Holwood was the prime minister's favourite asylum from the excitement and turmoil of Westminster. Here, when weary of faction and debate, Mr Pitt retired for relaxation and rest. There is still remaining near Holwood House a fine oak, known as "Pitt's Oak," under which it was the premier's habit to sit and read. The tree stands upon a conical mound which has at one time probably been a portion of the entrenchments of the old camp which Mr Pitt's schemes of gardening made it necessary to remove.

Holwood derives much of its interest from having been the residence for several years of the Rt. Hon. William Pitt. The house in which that eminent statesman lived was destroyed when the present elegant Grecian mansion was built. The exact spot upon which it stood is uncertain, but there is some ground for thinking that the lawn close to the present house covers the spot.

Nearer to Keston Church is an old tree called "Wilberforce's Oak." Under it is a stone seat bearing the following inscription :— "From Mr. Wilberforce's Diary, 1788. 'At length, I well remember after a conversation with Mr. Pitt in the open air at the root of an old tree at Holwood, just above the steep descent into the vale of Keston, I resolved to give notice on a fit occasion in the House of Commons of my intention to bring forward the abolition of the slave trade.' Erected by Earl Stanhope, 1862. By permission of Lord Cranworth."

In 1802 Sir George Pocock purchased Holwood from Mr Pitt for the sum of £15,000. Mr John Ward becoming possessed of the property in 1823, the old house was demolished, and the modern mansion was built in the year 1825, from the designs of

Decimus Burton. It has been said that although the rooms are not large, the architect has constructed at Holwood one of the most ornamental, convenient, and substantial mansions in this country.

Mr Brassey purchased the estate upon Mr Ward's death, and sold it in 1855 to the Rt. Hon. Lord Cranworth, Lord High Chancellor of England, a man of great personal popularity, and of whom it has been said that he was "fair and equal to all." He twice held the Great Seal of England, and had a seat on the Judicial Bench for twenty years. He died in 1868, and his remains rest beside those of Lady Cranworth in Keston churchyard. Robert Alexander, Esq., C.B., was Holwood's next owner, and soon after the estate became the property of its present noble owner, the Rt. Hon. the Earl of Derby.

Ancient Trees.

To the *Gentleman's Magazine* of September 1832 J. A. K. (*i.e.*, Mr J. A. Kempe) contributed an account of an ancient oak found buried in the little valley which runs through Keston Common. He says, "On endeavouring to dig it out, it proved to be the trunk of an oak, and, on sinking about ten feet through a compact stratum of fine white sand, they found the nether end resting on a bed of blue clay, filled in a very large proportion with fragments of white shells, minutely fractured, and so much decomposed as to crumble into dust at the touch. The trunk of the tree inclined at the angle of about 70 degrees towards the S.E. Several branches and detached portions were found at the surface of the land at a short distance. The trunk itself appeared to have turned root uppermost, and in that position to have been overwhelmed in the sand. It is about eleven feet in length, five in circumference, and the reversed end had been abruptly fractured. The wood is perfectly sound, stained by the soil of a bluish grey colour; the bark is a jet black, and in a carbonaceous state."

Upon the highest point of Keston Common, near Cæsar's Well, and on the east side of the gravel pit, a large quantity of charred oak was recently exposed in the side of the gravel pit, and not quite a foot from the surface. The spot is well suited for a beacon fire, and in these charred fragments of wood we have probably remains of such a fire, answering to other fires on the high ground of Shooter's Hill and Shirley Common.

Keston Church.

From the Archdeacon's Well it is but a short distance to Keston Church. Five minutes' walk along a pleasant lane, and down a steep hill past Keston Court Farm, brings the rambler to a fine avenue of old pollard elms about thirty in number. Keston Church, embowered in elm trees, is just beyond that avenue. It is a building which has no claim to grandeur; on the contrary, it is small and insignificant. But to an antiquary it is of great interest. It consists only of a chancel and nave, with vestry and porch. The chancel, which is quite small, measuring internally about twenty feet by seventeen feet, has walls of flint about two feet six inches in thickness, pierced on the north and south sides by four narrow cusped lancet windows (two in each side) of about the time of Henry III. In the east wall, above the altar, is a quite modern window designed to match the lancets in the side walls. The chancel arch is very heavy and massive, about two feet four inches thick, and quite plain, with unornamented stone imposts. Its span is thirteen feet six inches, and its shape pointed. Of the nave, measuring internally forty-nine feet six inches in length, and eighteen feet nine inches in breadth, little can now be made out, as the walls have been cased externally with flint work, and are now two feet six inches or more in thickness, and no signs of the original windows are visible. The only nave windows of any antiquity are extremely ugly, and date probably from the middle or latter part of the eighteenth century, or still later; but their exact age is a point of little importance. I believe the nave to be of Norman workmanship, but the characteristics of the original nave walls, remains of windows, &c., are covered by the external flint casing, and it is beneath that that we should have to look for fully confirmatory evidence of this theory.

However there are some interesting remains inside the church which seem to show that this theory is probable. At the east end of the nave's south wall there is an arch now filled in with masonry. Its size is sufficiently large to suggest that it was intended to give access to a transept or chapel. The arch is visible outside as well as inside, but as no other indications of such a building are apparent, it seems probable that the arch was constructed with a view to the future addition of a transept or chapel. Very possibly the building contemplated was a chantry chapel, and the original design may have been abandoned after the decease of he whom it was to commemorate.

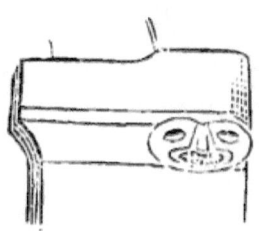

The western jamb of this filled-in arch has for its impost a very curious and interesting specimen of early Norman carving. At a glance it is evident that the stone is not in its original position. That part of it which ought to fit flush against the wall is rounded at the corner, and was intended to be in an exposed place. There can be but small room to doubt that it is a relic of a former building here, and it is probable that that building was a church built in the early part of the eleventh century. The lower portion of the chancel arch and some portions at least of the nave walls may probably date to the same period. On the side of the stone is a very quaint representation of a human face, very broad, with lizard eyes, and the mouth, broad and grinning, stuck full of teeth. The late Professor J. H. Parker, C.B., of Oxford (with whom the writer had some correspondence in reference to the carving), pronounced it "early Norman work, probably of the time of William the Conqueror." The demoniac grin and distended cheeks remind one of the grotesque heads, symbolic of the festivities connected with Whitsun ales, which in mediæval times were carved in churches, &c. (At Smarden Church, for instance. See *Archæologia Cantiana*, Vol. xiv., pp. 29, 30.) The carving has been kept very perfect by a thick deposit of whitewash, under which for many years it had been hidden. At the restoration of the church in 1877 the whitewash was carefully removed, and the curious carving still remains in the church, interesting as a specimen of Norman art, and valuable as a relic of the church which, there is good reason to believe, existed at Keston at the time of the Conquest.

Parish Church Goods.

The following is an inventory of the Parish Church Goods at Keston, taken in the year 1552:—

KESTON—xxiii November. vi. Ed. VI.

Robert Barrett, parson; Thomas Comfort, churchwarden.

First one chalice with the patent of silver weying vi ounces and iij quarters.

Item ij small bells of brasse suted in the steple, on handbell of brasse, & one smale sacrying bell.

Item on crosse cloth of lynnen painted.

Item iij banner clothes of lynnen clothe painted, & iij staves to them belonging.

Item on surplesse, and one rochett of lynnen clothe, and one funte cloth of lynnen.

Item one old dyaper towell, & ij other of playne clothe.

Item ij alter clothes one of diaper & thother of playne clothe, & an olde alter clothe to hange before the Alter of threde & silke wrought together.

Item one crysmatory of latten, one crosse of copper & gilte with a staff belonging therto.

Bells.

There is one old bell at Keston bearing the following inscription and date:—

THOMAS · BARTLET · MADE · ME 1621.

It may be noted that "ij small bells of brasse" are mentioned in the inventory made in 1552. It is very possible that they may have been recast as one bell in 1621.

The "sacrying bell," mentioned in the same inventory, was doubtless only a small handbell. It was used in the Office of the Mass to warn people that the Elevation was about to take place.

The bell made by Bartlet in 1621 was kept in a small bell-cot on the west gable of the nave until 1880, when the church was restored, and a new open bell-cot built. In 1887 the Countess of Derby presented to the church a carillon of six bells, manufactured by Messrs Lewis & Co., organ-builders, of Brixton, and formerly bell-founders. The bells bear no inscription. Accommodation has been found for them by enlarging the bell-cot.

When the writer first visited Keston Church, above twenty years ago, the appearance of the church greatly differed from the appearance it now presents. There was a ceiled roof to the nave, supported by rough-hewn king posts, and there was a ceiled roof to the chancel. The seats, or rather "pews," of deal were lofty in height and bald in appearance. The pulpit also was high, and above it was a ponderous sounding board, in the middle of which was the figure in relief of a dove carved in wood, and the entire structure was *grained*. On either side of the Communion table was a dusky oil painting, representing probably Moses and Aaron. The east window in the chancel was a bare, bald stonework arrangement, Romanesque in design, and of a very unpleasing effect. It is reported to have come from Mr Pitt's old house at Holwood when that was demolished. Everything is now altered, thanks to the generosity and zeal of the rectors and parishioners of Keston. The roofs of both the chancel and nave are now of substantial open timber work. The hideous old pulpit is removed. The sounding board (quite unnecessary in such a small building) has disappeared, and the old pews have been replaced by comfortable benches.

The Communion table possesses the interesting feature of an elaborate cross, inlaid with variously coloured woods. About the middle of the cross are the words "The Keston Marke," and at the base is the motto "In hoc signo vinces." (In this sign thou shalt conquer.) At each corner of the table is a smaller cross. When the church was restored (1877) the Communion table was found to be in a very decayed state, and it was found necessary to replace the legs and some other parts, but the inlaid part was of course preserved. The thirty-sixth volume of *Archæologia* contains a paper by Mr G. R. Corner, wherein reference to it is made thus:—"The Communion table of oak is inlaid with a device formed of different woods, in the form of a cross *bottonée*; underneath which is written 'The Keston Mark,' and 'In hoc signo vinces.' The table is of the seventeenth century, and the device upon it seems to indicate that the clergy of that day sought to divert the thoughts of the people from a superstitious notion about the Keston Mark to the Christian Mark of the Cross."—*Archæologia*, Vol. xxxvi., p. 127. A woodcut of the device will be found at the end of that paper.

MONUMENTAL INSCRIPTIONS WITHIN KESTON CHURCH.

SANCTUARY.

On a grey ledger-stone.
Jane the wife of the
Reverend James Hodgson
Rector of this Parish
died February 15th 1790
Aged 36.
John Hodgson
died June 12th 1782
Aged 4.
James Hodgson
died Jany 5th 1791
Aged 14.
Elizabeth Ann Hodgson
died Jany 19th 1794.
Aged nine Weeks.

On a blue ledger-stone.

Here lyeth the Bodies of Judith
and Elizabeth the Wives of Capt
Richard Perch of Hollwoods
hill in this Parish who Deceased
the Former in the Month of June
1683 the Latter on the 23rd Day of
December in the year of our Lord
1704.

CHANCEL.

On a blue ledger-stone.

Here lyeth the body of
Jane
the Relict of
Edmund Smith
of London G^{ent} and Daughter
of Thomas Pyke
late Rector of this Church who departed
this life the ninth of December
Anno Dom. 1701
Æta 61

—

NOTE.—Near this stone are three other stones, but the inscriptions upon them are now hidden by the benches.

On the north wall of the Chancel is a well-carved marble relief and the following inscription:—

To the memory of George Kirkpatrick of
Hollydale, in this Parish, Esqr. of the Honble East India
Company's Civil Service, eldest son of the late
Colonel James Kirkpatrick of the Madras Army,
Born at Madras 2nd June A.D. 1762, Died at Hollydale 16th
March A.D. 1838.

NAVE.

A descent of these steps leads from the Chancel to the Nave, and close to the bottom step is a large slab of Bethersden stone, 7 feet 2 inches long, and from 2 feet 11 inches at the head tapering to 2 feet 7 inches at the foot. An incised cross *fleurie* on a recessed base occupies the chief part. Under the transverse limbs are two shield-shaped depressions, and there are remains of an incised marginal inscription in Lombardic characters. In the *Gentleman's Magazine* for November 1830 is the following account of it:—

"J. A. Kempe, Esq., F.S.A., communicated (to the Soc. of Antiq.) a sketch of a grave-stone, formerly ornamented by a cross fleury and two shields of brass, in Keston Church, Kent; together with a notice of the life of Sir Robert Belknap, Justice of the Common Pleas, who having suffered a sentence of banishment to Ireland in the 11th of Richard II., was recalled ten years after. Sir Robert was Lord of the manor of Keston, and Mr. Kempe has decyphered part of the inscription to be the words, REVENVE DE IRELANDE IADIE . . . . ."

On a grey ledger-stone.

Here lieth the body of
Mr. Duncomb Colchester
who Departed this Life
November the 17th 1746
Aged 42 Years.

On a grey ledger-stone.

Mrs. Alice Kay
Sister to the Rev^d
Arthur Kay who
Dyed June ye 17th 1761
Aged 44 years.

On a blue ledger-stone.

Beneath this Stone
Lieth the Body of Mrs. Jane Greene
Wife of Mr. Thos Greene of Sackvil
Street St James Westr who departed
this life the 21st of June 1710 aged 50.

On a blue ledger-stone with arms.

Here lieth the Body of the
Revd Christopher Clarke M.A.
Arch-deacon of Norwich,
Prebendary of Ely &
Rector of this Parish
He died the 19th of May 1742
Aged 70.

War Bank.

In Roman times War Bank was the site of a small village. Its distance from London corresponds very nearly with that of the first station (called Noviomagus) on the Roman road from London to Dover. Hence some suppose that the Roman buildings at War Bank represent that station; but others, seeing difficulties in the way of that theory, have preferred other localities. Camden thought Woodcote in Surrey a probable site. Other antiquaries have suggested several places in Kent. It is not the object of this account to settle so grave a dispute. Let us pass on to the remains of antiquity found at War Bank.

In 1854 Mr George R. Corner unearthed in the middle of Lower War Bank Field, and only eighteen inches below the surface of the ground, the foundations of a small Roman Villa, and in other parts of the same field he found walls and pavements of flintwork and concrete. Twenty-seven years before this, in 1827, Mr Thomas Crofton Croker excavated the circular foundations (still visible) of a supposed temple of Roman date, and found in a grave eight feet deep a massive stone coffin of an equally early period. Shortly after this Mr A. J. Kempe uncovered the remains of a square edifice, probably a tomb, from which a stone coffin had been taken, and several other traces of Roman occupation. In the *Gentleman's Magazine* for May 1829 he has described and figured several curious relics found by him in his three weeks' researches at War Bank. Among them are the following objects—brass ear-ring, iron key, silver stylus, tongue of a brass fibula, sepulchral urns, and various fragments of pottery.

Dunkin's "History and Antiquities of Bromley," published in 1815, contains a chapter on Holwood Hill, illustrated by an etching of antiquities found there. The rough woodcut here given is copied from that etching, and represents an urn, partially broken, found in cleaning out a ditch at War Bank. When first found it contained ashes and calcined bones, showing its funereal origin.

FUNEREAL URN, WAR BANK.

The fictile remains found in this and the neighbouring fields are not dissimilar to those which are usually found scattered about the vicinity of Roman buildings. Broken tiles, both for bonding and roofing purposes, fragments of various culinary vessels, portions of the noses, sides and handles of amphoræ in rough yellow or drab ware, and some pieces of fine pottery, black or dark slate-coloured (doubtless from the extensive works at Upchurch in Kent), have from time to time been found turned up by the plough. A few broken pieces of unornamented Samian ware have also been found. Mr Kempe mentions some pottery "studded with pebbles from the gravel, not bigger than mustard seed," which he supposed to be in imitation of mosaic work. This was doubtless a part of a mortarium or mortar used in crushing grain, and the minute pebbles partially imbedded in the vessel were designed to assist in the process of crushing. The present writer found a similar fragment a few years ago. Quite recently he has found some pieces of flint chipped into forms which suggest that they were the teeth or spikes of a tribulum, or machine for separating grain from the straw. This idea has every appearance of probability when we remember how necessary appliances for thrashing and crushing grain would be in a small country village such as War Bank was in Roman times.

Coins are very scarce; but Mr Corner has been able to give the following list of coins found at War Bank.

        Clodius Albinus.
        Victorinus (?)
        Claudius Gothicus.
        Allectus.
        Carausius.
        Constantinus Magnus.

(For fuller particulars of the coins see *Archaeologia*, Vol. xxxvi., p. 123.)

In the year 1882 a small terra-cotta lamp was found near the residence of Lady Caroline Legge. When turned up by the gardener's spade it was supposed to be a quaint kind of cream jug. It is now in the possession of the writer. It is nearly perfect, wanting only a small part of the handle. Its length is 4¾ inches, and its breadth is only 2¼ inches, thus it has a rather longer shape than is usual in Roman lamps. It is made of fine terra-cotta, and is probably of foreign manufacture. Marks of wear appear on the underside of the lamp, caused doubtless by friction with the disc of the candelabrum.

Several Roman buildings seem to have existed in the neighbourhood of War Bank. Mr Corner mentions the existence of foundations (presumably of Roman age) under the surface of a field at Baston. In Gates Green, not more than a mile distant, in a western direction, from War Bank, I have seen, turned up by the plough, Roman bonding tiles of nearly full size, with fragments of hard mortar still adhering to them, and near the farmhouse at Rowes Farm I have found several fragments of pottery of unquestionably Roman date. In digging out the foundations for the north aisle of Hayes Church some years ago there was found a solid mass of mortar containing a large proportion of pounded tile—a true characteristic of Roman mortar—and several tiles of Roman age have been built into the flint work of the tower and walls of Hayes Church, where they remain to this day. Their presence suggests that a Roman building or foundations were hard by when those parts of the Church were erected.

From these facts it will appear probable that many buildings were dotted about this district in Roman times, although their foundations are now buried beneath a great depth of earth which the cultivation of the land and the influences of rain, &c., have brought down from higher levels.

There is little evidence to show how the little village at War Bank fell into desuetude, or whether it was destroyed suddenly or succumbed to gradual decay; but the presence of charcoal among the ruins suggests that fire was the agent by which it was destroyed. The old people of Keston still imagine that the green turf of War Bank covers treasure of untold value.

WEST WICKHAM.

WEST WICKHAM.

The name Wickham is probably derived from the Anglo-Saxon words *wic*, a street or way, and *ham*, a dwelling. The parish, which contains about two thousand five hundred acres of land, borders upon Surrey, and the boundary between it and that county is marked by a narrow belt of woodland known as Kent Gate. The ground does not appear to have been cultivated at any time. Probably it was a sort of neutral land anciently known as a "mark," from the Anglo-Saxon mearce, which means a mark or boundary. There are, in this neighbourhood, several traces of marks, as at Keston, where the popular name of a public house, "Keston Mark," on the boundary of Keston parish, remains to this day. Kent Gate, under the name "Cinta Stiogole," Kent style or gate, is mentioned in an Anglo-Saxon charter, dated A.D. 862. In 1797, according to Hasted's account, there were in West Wickham about seventy houses, and about twenty acres of waste land.

Parish Church.

The builders of West Wickham Church, whoever they may have been, must have been persons possessed of considerable artistic taste. Few more beautiful sites could be found anywhere in the parish than that which the church occupies, although it is of course very likely that its selection was influenced to some

WEST WICKHAM CHURCH.

extent by the necessity of it being near to the Manor-house, for purposes of both safety and convenience.

The plan of the structure is rather singular and not remarkable either for beauty or convenience, but this is due to the building of a north aisle in 1844. The chancel and Lady-chapel were probably erected about the end of the 15th century. The rest of the church dates from the year 1844, when, besides the addition of a north aisle, the church was considerably rebuilt. There is very little in the construction of the walls which calls for remark, excepting, perhaps, the massive pier on the north side of the chancel-arch, which has been considered by Sir Stephen

Glynne as of earlier date than the other parts of the church. Sir Stephen Glynne visited the church in 1833, and it is very likely that when he made his notes there was more opportunity of judging of the relative ages of the masonry. As present, both the pier in question and the old walls of the church, internally and externally, are too much covered by cement to allow one to pronounce any very definite opinion on the matter. This is much to be regretted, as the walls are extremely likely to contain some relics of a still earlier church than that built in the latter part of the 15th century, of which the chancel and Lady-chapel remain. The existence of such an earlier building is well known, and proved by early records and monumental remains inside and outside of the existing church. It may be added that Sir Stephen Glynne mentions the existence of some remains of vaulting in the tower. No traces of them are to be seen now; probably they disappeared in 1844.

Leland thus speaks of the building of West Wickham Church and Wickham Court:—

"Henry Sunne to John (Heydon), passid not of the Gaines of the Law, or to any great Getting by Service, but al for profite at Home. And yet he did great Feates . . . . He purchased 300 Markes of Land yn yerely Rent. Whereof an Hunderith *li* by yere is at Wikam by Lewsham in Surrey, towards Croydon, wher he buildid a right fair Manor Place, and a fair Chirche." (*Itinerary of John Leland the Antiquary*, 1710-11, Vol. iv., fol. 15.)

It may be remarked that the nave is entered by descending three or four steps from the porch under the tower. The church is dedicated to St John the Baptist, and it has been suggested that this arrangement was intended to illustrate St John iii. 30—"He must increase, but I must decrease." It is, however, quite possible that the sloping nature of the ground had more to do with the low level of the nave than the reason given by this fanciful explanation.

The dimensions of the church are, roughly, as follows:—

Internal Measurements.

    Nave, 34 ft. 1 in. by 21 ft. 6 in.
    North Aisle, 27 ft. 8 in. by 24 ft. 4 in.
    Western Recess, 9 ft. 10 in. by 4 ft. 6 in.
    Chancel, 28 ft. by 19 ft.
    Lady Chapel, 28 ft. by 12 ft.
    Tower (porch), 11 ft. 10 in. by 11 in. ft. 10.
    Vestry, 8 ft. 8 in. by 9 ft.

External Measurements.

    Tower, 19 ft. by 19 ft.; 48 ft. high.

On the south wall of the nave, close to the Communion table, is a piscina of very plain and unornamented character, and on the north wall, nearly opposite, is an ambry or locker, of which, although the door is wanting, the iron hinge-hooks and the staple for holding the bolt still remain. Another piscina exists on the south wall of the Lady-chapel. The depression or basin which conducted the water to the drain-pipe is elegantly carved in a six-foiled shape.

Monuments.

There are three monumental brasses in West Wickham Church. The oldest commemorates "Dominus" William De Thorp, a

Rector of the parish, who died in 1407. The title "Dominus" was often given merely in a complimentary way to the clergy, and it was probably bestowed in this way upon the priest who is mentioned upon the brass. The figure is very fine, and displays considerable skill in the execution, but it is chiefly valuable as a good specimen of the ecclesiastical costume of the day. It has been preserved very well indeed, and is to be seen upon the floor at the west end of the chancel. The following is the inscription in abbreviated Latin.

"Hic jacet D'n's Will'm's De Thorp quonda' Rector istius Eccl'ie qui obiit decimo die Maii Anno d'ni M^{c}cccc Septimo cui' an'e propicietur deus AMEN."

Towards the east end of the chancel is another brass to a former Rector of the parish, "Sr." John Stockton. The effigy is much inferior to that just mentioned, and the stiffer style of dress also indicates a later date. The word "Sir" in the inscription is merely complimentary. The following inscription is engraved upon the brass :—

"Pray for the soule of Sr John' Stockton the whiche decessed the xxiiii day of september ye yer of o'lord M^{o}V^{c}XV o'whose soule ih'u have m'ci."

On the south wall of the chancel is a brass tablet engraved with the following inscription :—

JOHN LANG BORNE AT RICHMOND IN YE COVNTY OF YORKE WAS AFTERWARDE ONE OF THE FELLOWES OF ST. IOHNS COL: IN CAMBRIDGE, BY THE SPACE OF IX YEARES ; FROM THENCE HE WAS LAWFVLLY & FREELY CALLED TO BE PARSON OF THIS PARISH OF WESTWICKHAM, WHERE HE CONTINVED RESIDENT THE WHOLE TIME OF XXXIJ YEARES AND MORE WHO LIVED HELRE WITH THE GOOD REPORT &

LIKINGE OF THOSE Yt DID FEARE GOD & IN AN ASSVRED HOPE OF A BETTER LIFE AFTER THIS IN YE KINGDOME OF HEAVEN; THIS MEMORIALL OF HIM WAS MADE IN A° 1619 AN IN THE 77TH YEARE OF HIS AGE.

As the date of death is not mentioned, it is very probable that this inscription was written during the lifetime of John Lang.

Near the south door of the church there is a slab of stone which has evidently contained a brass. From the depression which was originally made to receive the brass, it was clear, some two or three years ago, that the brass consisted of an oblong tablet for the inscription, and the demi-figure of a priest of small size. Judging from the brass to John Osteler in Hayes Church, to which it bore considerable similarity, the date may be fixed approximately at about the middle or latter half of the fifteenth century. The matrix has suffered considerably from exposure to the weather, and it is now very difficult to make out much of the former shape of the brass from the marks which remain upon the stone.

Near the south door are also some fragments of a large limestone slab bearing portions of a marginal inscription in Lombardic characters. I have not succeeded in deciphering more than a word or two of the inscription, nor in identifying it with any inscription in Thorpe's "Registrum Roffense."

Upon the floor of the Lady-chapel is an early slab, probably of Bethersden marble, which presents several features in common with that in memory of Sir Robert Belknap, at Keston Church. It appears to have possessed, originally, a cross-flory in brass, and a marginal inscription which Mr Waller, the well-known antiquary, reads as follows:—

"Sire Wauter : de : Hontingfeld : Chivaler : gist : icy : Deu : de : sa : alme : eyt : merci."

It was the tomb of Sir Walter de Huntingfield, who obtained the grant of an annual fair for West Wickham on the eve and festival of Saint Mary Magdalene.

A curious marble tomb exists on the south wall of the Lady-chapel. The central figure is a seated lady, with one hand resting upon a clasped book lying upon a square table. At her feet is the figure of a young child clad in grave-clothes or swaddling-clothes. This is the tomb of Margaret, wife of Thomas Hobbes, Esq., eldest daughter of Sir Samuel Lennard. She died in child-bed of her only child, in 1608, aged 20. Below the carved figures is a Latin inscription as follows:—

> Margaritæ uxoris Tho : Hobbes Arm^ri : primogenitæ Sam^lis : Lennard Mil^s : 20 : plus annos natæ ex abortu filioli sui unici (hic unâ sepulti) 20 : Febr : A° D'ni : 1608 : ex morte ad vitam translatæ corpus hic obdormit. In cujus erga Deum pietatis, in parentes conjugemque, amoris et obsequii gemmæ vere splendidæ, piam memoriam : lugubris conjux indignum hoc monumentum posuit.

Some arms upon this monument are thus described by Thorpe, in *Registrum Roffense*: "Argent, a bend wavy, azure, between two birds of the same (as I think); impaling four coats quarterly: first, Or, on a fesse gules three fleurs-de-lis of the field; secondly, quarterly argent and sable, an eagle displayed of the last in the first quarter; thirdly, Vaire, argent and sable, a chief ermine; fourth, as the first."

At the east end of the Lady-chapel is a marble altar-tomb covered by a slab of black marble. Above it are the Lennard arms, Or, on a fesse gu. three fleurs-de-lis of the field, a crescent for difference, and the following inscription:—

Memoriæ Samuelis Lennardi, militis charissimi mariti posuit mœstissima conjunx Elisabetha: Is Cheveningo oriundus, Cantabrigiæ & Lincolniensis hospitii alumnus; Westwickhamiæ, ubi sedem fixit terræ redditus ——[1] & ——[1] fuit Christianæ veritatis zelo, Romani vero pseudo-christianismi & bigeneris religionis odio flagravit: ex præfata Elizabetha, Stephani Slanye, militis, nuper maioris civitatis London filiarum una filios habuit quatuor filiasque octo. Obiit anno ætatis sexagesimo quinto ineunte, eræ Christianæ 1618. Aprilis primo.

INTERIOR OF WEST WICKHAM CHURCH.

Among numerous other monumental inscriptions are memorials of the following:

Harriet, Countess of Devon, died 1839.

Sir John Farnaby, Baronet, died 1802.

[1] Two Greek words, meaning "a lover of learning, and a lover of virtue."

Sir Charles Francis Farnaby, Baronet, died 1859, and several members of the Farnaby and Cator families.

Gilbert West, died 1756, and other members of the West family.

Admiral George Augustus Eliott, died 1872.

ROODSCREEN.

The roodscreen still exists, in the church, dividing the chancel from the nave and the Lady-chapel from the north aisle. The date assigned to the screen is about the year 1500. Its architectural merits are considerable. The linen pattern in the lower panels and the tracery in the upper open panels are both very good. The ornament upon the shafts of the screen is remarkable as being exactly similar to some of the details of the elegant rood screen in Lullingstone Church, Kent, which has been shown by Canon Scott Robertson to have been designed between 1502 and 1520. The screen at West Wickham occupies its original place, and over the entrance to the chancel may still be seen the socket in which the rood, or large crucifix, was formerly fastened. As was the usual custom in all parochial churches, the chancel and altar, are enclosed only by an open screen. The object of this arrangement was to allow the worshippers in the body of the church to see the priest at the altar. In large conventual and collegiate churches and cathedrals, on the other hand, the choirs were generally enclosed by a solid screen of stone or woodwork, for security from draughts and noises arising from persons moving about in the open parts of the church. Roodscreens are still to be found in about thirty Kentish churches. At Shoreham Church, in the same county, the roodloft still exists in situ.

There is some ancient oak panelling near the communion table. The pulpit has some carved oaken panels of later date than the roodscreen. Probably their date is about the time of Queen Anne. The framework of the pulpit, and reading-desk is quite modern.

Bells.

Five bells of melodious tone hang in the tower. The following are their inscriptions:—

    I. Gloria . Deo . in . excelsis . 1640 . B.E.
    II. C & G Mears Founders London 1857.
    III. *O . John . Hodson . made . mee . 1669 . Edward Wooden . Church . Warden . . WH . CH . . .
    IV. Brianvs . Eldredge . me . fecit . 1624
    V. Gloria . Deo . in . Excelsis.
        Bryanvs . Eldridge . made . mee . 1640.

As will be observed from the inscriptions, the first, fourth, and fifth bells were cast by Bryan Eldridge. The motto " Gloria Deo in excelsis " was invariably used upon bells cast by this founder during the last ten years of his life. The foundry at which he cast his bells generally was situated at Chertsey, in Surrey. It appears to have been a flourishing institution, and existed for upwards of a century. It has been suggested, however, that the Kentish bells, founded by Eldridge, were not cast at Chertsey, but locally where they now exist.

Peals are rung on the bells at West Wickham Church on New

    * A coin of Charles II. is here inserted in the bell.

Year's Eve, Queen's Birthday and Coronation, and on 29th May, and 5th November.

Painted Glass.

The windows of the Lady-chapel are adorned with some beautiful painted glass of the latter part of the fifteenth century. Mr J. G. Waller, F.S.A., thus writes:—Half a century ago " this chapel was particularly interesting. On the wall hung a helmet, beneath which was an ancient gauntlet and short sword, perhaps of the fifteenth century, and suspended from the roof were several funeral banners emblazoned with arms, all tattered, worn and dusty. Around were the beautiful remains of painted glass, all of which I carefully traced; and I have recollections of my solitary task in autumn days and waning light, as having very solemn surroundings. This glass . . . has suffered during the last half century, and lost some of its beauty, which is now chiefly preserved in my tracings." The ancient armour, banners, and several shields of arms (particulars of which may be found in Thorpe's *Registrum Roffense*) have been removed from the church. " Collectors of curiosities," as Hone sarcastically remarks, " paid their attentions to these windows, and carried off specimens." The spoilers have, however, left the glass illustrating more or less completely eight different subjects, of which the following are brief particulars.

East Window.

The Virgin and Child. The Virgin Mary has long, flowing, auburn hair, and wears a crown and sceptre in token of her imperial character as Queen of Heaven. The infant Christ holds a dove, the emblem of love, innocence, meekness, and purity, and here represented probably in allusion to the customary offering of a pair of doves or pigeons upon the occasion of the purification of women, according to the Jewish law.

Kneeling Skeleton, and arms. Mr Waller considers the skeleton to be a representation of Henry Heydon, rebuilder of the church, in 1480. The arms are those of Heydon. There is a scroll near the figure upon which is written, "Ne reminiscaris domine delicta nostra nec delicta nostrorum parentum," from the passage in the Litany, "Remember not, Lord, our offences, nor the offences of our forefathers, &c."

St. Christopher bearing Christ. The name Christopher signifies Christ-bearer, and has reference to the legend of the saint, who carried people over a river with the view of performing some good and meritorious work. One day a child cried to be carried across, but the weight was so great as to make the saint, when he arrived at the opposite shore, say that he had never before had so heavy a weight. "Wonder not," said the child, "for you have borne the Creator of the world."

St. Anne teaching the Virgin. This is a very popular subject in mediæval ecclesiastical art, although wholly unwarranted by historical evidence. The figure of the Virgin is pretty, and the ermine trimmings are remarkable, being designed, no doubt, to symbolise her royal descent.

North Windows.

The *Mater Dolorosa*. This is a very beautiful relic of mediæval art. The drawing is well executed, and the treatment of the subject altogether displays a high degree of merit. Mr Waller says, "The artist who designed this had no common mind, but his name is in oblivion. There is nothing superior to it in the boasted glass of Fairford."

St Dorothea. This subject represents the saint with long flowing golden hair, encircled by a chaplet of roses, and holding in one hand a basket of the same, and with the other offering one to an infant figure of Christ, whose hands are uplifted to receive it. The simple grace of the composition is well worthy attention and study.

St Catherine of Alexandra. This is a full-length figure of the saint, crowned, and with the head encircled with a glory. She has long flowing robes, over which falls her long unfettered hair, the sign of a maiden. Her left hand holds a book and a large sword, the handle of which is richly ornamented. At the saint's feet lies the prostrate figure of the Emperor Maxentius, crowned, and with a sceptre or mace in his left hand. His right hand rests upon a wheel armed with knives or sharp spikes, which appears in the background. Alban Butler thus relates the incident:—" She (St. Catherine) is said first to have been put upon an engine composed of four wheels joined together, and stuck with sharp pointed spikes, that when the wheels were moved she might be torn in pieces. . . . At the first stirring of the terrible engine the cords with which the martyr was tied were broken asunder by the invisible hand of an angel, and she was delivered from that death. . . ." She was at length beheaded.

St Christopher. This is not entirely original glass, but has been patched up, as indeed have most of the windows, with more or less modern glass. There are, or were, some remnants of an original diaper of I. H. C. forming a background to the various subjects. This has now been reproduced in modern work, and used in filling-in the spaces around the mediæval figures.

There are some ancient encaustic tiles at the east end of the chancel in front of the communion rails, but they are so much worn that the pattern upon some of them is destroyed. Among those which are the least worn is an elegant example of the fleur-de-lis; others bear circles, fine-petalled flowers, and other designs. They are of two sizes, five inches square, and four and a half inches square.

Parish Church Goods.

The following is an inventory of Parish Church Goods made in 1552:—

   West Wykham—xxiii November vi Ed. VI.
  John Brigett and Robert Cawstone, churchwardens.

First one chalice of copper all gilt with a patente of silver parcell gilte waying ij ounes.

Item on other chalice with the patente of silver and parcell gilt waying x ounes.

Item a pix of latten with a lynnen cloth thereto made after a net facion.

Item a crismatory and on cruett of pewder.

Item a crosse of latten with a crosse staffe half latten.

Item iij litle towells for thalter, a cope of red silke with a border with images imbrothered with silke.

Item ij candlestikks for thalter of latten whereof one broken.

Item a bible of the greatest volume, and a paraphrasis of Erasmus.

Item iiij grete bells suted in the steple, and a Saints bell of brasse.

Item on holy water stoppe of latten.

[Endorsed] Dertforde xxiij November vj Ed. Vi. Memorandum:

All goods in the inventory of iij Ed. VI. are in this, and are now delivered to the churchwardens to answer the same

"Except iij corprax cases a vestment of tawney vellet a vestment of blewe silke a vestment of grene sarcenett on cruell ij old alter clothes of diaper iiij playne alter clothes a frunt clothe of grene and red satten a bridgs a frunt cloth of white silk iiij towells a cope of red silk with silk hangyng a border of blewe satten a cloth for weddings and churchings ij surplesses a litle surples for the clark presented unto the saide Commyssioners by thothes of the said churchwardens to be stollen and also except one chalice with a patent of silver parcell gilte that was broken waying xj ounces di presented to be sold by the saide churchwardens with the consent of the parishoners there and employed about the necessarie reparacious of the parish church."

The "Saints bell of brasse" mentioned in the above inventory was doubtless the sanctus bell. This was generally placed in a little bellcote by itself on the gable of the chancel roof, and was rung three times when the priest said the *Sanctus* in the Office of the Mass. The object in placing the bell on the chancel gable, or between it and the nave, or in the belfry if that happened to be near the altar, was that the bell-rope hanging from it might be within easy reach of the server at the altar. It was placed outside the church, so that its tones might be heard all around, and all might join in the holy song of adoration. The West Wickham sanctus bell probably had a bellcote above the chancel gable.

Charities.

On a large black wooden tablet fixed to the east wall of the north aisle are the following particulars of "Benefactions to this Parish":—

"The Lady Margaret Slaney in the year 1610 gave three Pounds p. ann. to the poor of this parish payable by the Grocers' Company.

"In memory of the execrable Gunpowder Plot, Sir Samuel Lennard, Bart., in the year 1617 gave 20 shillings p. ann. to the Minister to preach on the 5th of November and 40 shillings to 40 poor people, viz., 15 of this Parish, 10 of Keston, 10 of Haies, and 5 of Farnborough, who are all to be present to hear the Sermon.

"The land in Haies called Dockmead is charg'd with the payment of this money.

"Christopher Hussey, D.D., Rector.

"Mr George Phillips,} Churchwardens.
"Mr Gabriel Wood,   }

"In the year 1734."

This sermon is still preached on the 5th of November every year.

Parish Register.

The Parish Register dates from the year 1558. The entries before the year 1600 do not appear to be original; they are probably copies of separate older entries brought together at that time into the form of one volume. Mention is frequently made of burials "in woollen" between the years 1678 and 1705. Lysons, in his *Environs of London*, mentions that in 1603, one person died in this parish of the plague; in 1608, four; in 1609, two; in 1625, one; and in 1665 (the plague year), two.

Lich Gate.

The lich gate forms a picturesque object at the east end of the churchyard. From the appearance of the timbers of which it is constructed, there is no doubt that it is of considerable antiquity. It is placed at the principal entrance to the churchyard, in accordance with the purpose for which it was built. The word "lich" signifies a corpse. We have an example of the use of the word in the name Lichfield = the Field of the Dead. The object of a lich gate was to afford shelter for the corpse and funeral party during the space which it might be necessary to wait for the officiating clergyman. It formed a decent place at which to wait, too, when the party arrived before the appointed hour, which, in large parishes where long journeys had to be performed on foot, not unfrequently occurred. King Edward VI.'s "Prayer Book," printed in 1549, directs, in the rubric of the Burial of the Dead, that "The priest meting the Corps at the Church style, shall say, &c."

West Wickham Court.

Hasted traces back the history of the manor of West Wickham to the time of Edward the Confessor, when it was held in fee simple of the king by one Godric. William the Confessor granted the manor to his half-brother Odo, Bishop of Bayeux. Adam Fitzhubert held it of the Bishop, as the survey of Domesday informs us. Therein it is entered under the general title of the Bishop of Bayeux's lands. The following is a translation of the entry.

"The same Adam holds of the bishop (of Bayeux) Wicheham. It was taxed at one suling. The arable land is . . . In demesne there are two carucates, and 24 villeins having four carucates. There are 13 servants, and one church, and one mill of 20 pence yearly value, and one wood for the pannage of 10 hogs. In the time of King Edward the Confessor it was worth 8 pounds, and afterwards 6 pounds, and now 13 pounds. Godric held it of King Edward."

The Manor came afterwards into the possession of the Huntingfields, an eminent Kentish family, seated here at West Wickham, and at Huntingfield in Eastling. From the Roll of Knights' Fees, taken in the seventh year of King Edward I., it appears that Peter de Huntingfield was then lord of West Wickham. He was named on the list of those brave Kentish gentlemen who attended that king in his victorious expedition into Scotland in the 26th year of his reign, and assisted at the siege of Carlaverock, in that kingdom; for which service he, with many others, received the honour of knighthood. He died in the seventh year of Edward II. His son and heir, Sir Walter de Huntingfield, next held the manor. He obtained, in the eleventh year of Edward II., a charter of free warren, a market weekly on Mondays, and a fair yearly on the vigil and day of St Mary Magdalene. He also had a license to impark his woods, called Frithwood, Ladywood, and Courtwood in the adjoining parish of Addington. He was buried in the parish church, and his monument still exists on the floor of the Ladychapel. His son, Sir John de Huntingfield, succeeded him. Before the end of the forty-second year of Edward III. this family terminated in two female heirs, Joane and Alice, the former of whom married John Copledike, and the latter Sir John Norwich. Upon the division of the inheritance, this manor was allotted to the elder daughter Joane. Her husband, John Copledike, possessed it in the last year of Richard II. In the seventeenth year of Henry VI., Thomas Squerie, of Squeries Court, Westerham, died possessed of the manor. His son John succeeded him, and died without issue in the fourth year of Edward IV. His younger sister, Dorothy, wife of Richard Mervin, of Fontels, Wiltshire, succeeded to the manor. Richard Scrope appears to have possessed it next, and, in the seventh year of Edward IV., alienated it by fine to Ambrose Crescacre, and he, not long after, transmitted it by sale to Henry Heydon, of Baconsthorpe, Norfolk, Esquire, and afterwards knighted. He built a considerable part of the manor-house, West Wickham Court, and re-built the church. Sir John Heydon, his son, inherited the manor, and left it at his death to Sir Christopher Heydon, his son, who was a man of some note in the reign of Queen Elizabeth. His son and heir, Sir William Heydon, who succeeded him, alienated the manor and estate by sale in the latter end of the reign of Queen Elizabeth to John Lennard, of Chevening, Esquire, who also possessing Knole at Sevenoaks, gave Wickham to his second son, Samuel. Sir Samuel Lennard was knighted, and his son, Sir Stephen, was created a baronet in 1642. Upon his death, his son, Sir Stephen, succeeded to the estate and manor. He died in 1709, leaving his wife, three daughters, and one son, Sir Samuel Lennard, Bart., who succeeded him. Upon the death of the last named baronet in 1727, he left no lawful issue, but to his two natural sons, Samuel and Thomas, he devised the former the manor, and the latter the advowson of the Church. From Samuel Lennard, Esq., the estate descended to his daughter Mary, who afterwards carried it in marriage to John Farnaby, Esq., afterwards Sir John Farnaby, Bart. From the last named it descended to his son, Sir Charles Francis Farnaby, Bart., who, dying in 1859, was succeeded by his nephew, John Farnaby Cator, who took the name of Lennard upon succeeding to the estate in 1861, and has since received the honour of a baronetcy.

When Sir Henry Heydon rebuilt the manor house, he constructed a building of a fortified nature, designed to resist the attacks of marauders or small forces of an enemy, but not capable of sustaining anything like a lengthy or regular siege. There were no external windows, except those in the four turrets, but there were windows looking into the courtyard which formerly existed inside of the house, and has now been roofed over and converted into a staircase. The present roof has at some time been raised about 20 inches higher than the original, with the evident object of gaining space. The house is a square brick building with an octagonal tower at each corner, which formerly terminated pyramidically above the roof, but are now flat. The walls are all embattled, with machicolations over the doorway. The present porch was built at about the time of Charles I. The heavy oak door at the main entrance is original, and has a curious lock and spring iron bars. The outer surface of the door has sometime been subjected to a severe battering which has left very clear marks. The "entresol" is a curious feature in the house, advantage having been taken of the lower ground on the west and north sides to obtain an extra floor, still retaining the ground floor. The kitchen was under the entresol: the underground offices are now used as cellars. The well was probably in the cellars, but it has long been disused. When the mullioned windows were inserted in the outside walls, extinguishers, after the French chateau style, were placed on the turrets. The ceilings throughout the house were originally constructed with heavy rough beams like the roof of the old dining-hall. Behind the present panelling in the drawing-room there are remains of still older panels. The fire dogs in this room are very beautiful, bearing the royal arms of England enamelled on copper in blue and white.

It is supposed, from the stags' heads in the dining-hall being all American, and from the original full-length portrait of Sir Walter Raleigh and his son being here, that some of the family accompanied Sir Walter in one or more of his expeditions to America. There are portraits here of Sir John Lennard, the founder of the Lennard family; Dr Farnaby, the scholar and grammarian, who founded the Farnaby family; Sir Sydney Stafford Smythe, a baron of the Exchequer, of the Strangford family, who married a Miss Farnaby; Prince George of Denmark, to whom Sir Samuel Lennard, Colonel of the Second Regiment of Horse Guards, was Equerry; Sir Samuel himself; the Earl of Sussex and his wife, Lady Anne Palmer, daughter of Charles II.; and of King Charles II., on the staircase, with others unknown.

In the hall are the following arms in painted glass:—Edward IV. and those of his Queen, Elizabeth Woodville; Duchess of York; Henry VIII., and Anne Boleyn, with her cypher; De Huntingfield; Copledyke; Scrope; Cressacre; Lennard. Other shields impale Lennard with Harman, Slaney, Leigh, Stanley of Alderley, Hale, Delalynd-Hussey, Carew of Beddington, Chadwick, Holmden, Bird, Weston, and Lambert. The quarterings 1 and 4 Lennard;

M

2 Byrde; 3 Bickworth, occur repeatedly on wood and on stone. Shields also appear with the arms of Heydon impaled with those of Boleyn, Brooke, Carew, and with unnamed coats.

The additions to West Wickham Court are in the style of a period about 120 years later than the original structure. The junction between the old and new parts is at one face of the south-east turret.

A paper on West Wickham Court was contributed by Sir John Farnaby Lennard, Bart., the present possessor, and lord of the manor, to the thirteenth volume of "Archæologia Cantiana."

EARTHWORKS.

Upon the high ground overlooking Coney Hall Farm there are some distinct remains of defensive earthworks. They have been considered by some to be of very early date, and possibly coeval with the pre-Roman Camp in Holwood Park. Camden, the antiquary, writing in 1610, says, "As for the other small intrenchment not farre of by *W. Wickham*, it was cast in fresh memorie when old *Sir Christopher Heydon*, a man of great command in these parts, trained the country people."—*Britannia*, 1610 edition, p. 326. In June 1879 several gentlemen, interested in the study of antiquities, conducted some excavations upon the site of the old earthworks, with the object of settling if possible the question as to the age of the works. On the southern side of the intrenchment the ditch is deep and well defined. On the west side it is broken by a gravel pit. Several lines of ditch and mound work can be traced out in a northern direction. A square mound, about eight feet high, is situated towards the southern end of the enclosure.

This looked as if it might have been originally a sepulchral barrow, and a trench was cut through it with the view of ascertaining whether there was any good ground for such a supposition. The trench was about two feet wide, eight feet deep, and thirty feet long. Every shovelful of earth as it was thrown out of the trench was carefully examined, but no antiquarian remains were found. The section through the mound, revealed by the trench, showed the whole of it to have been artificially built up of the ordinary pebble beds so plentiful at Hayes Common. The material of which it was composed was probably excavated from the deep ditch already mentioned. Upon the original surface of the ground there was a bed of sand of peculiar whiteness, probably due to an admixture with vegetable ash. It is probable that this was the deposit of a fire of rubbish made when the ground was cleared for the construction of the earthworks. There is a local tradition which asserts that this is the site of an old beacon. For such a purpose the prominent height of the spot would be peculiarly suitable, as from it all the high points of ground for many miles round are clearly visible. No fragments of charcoal or other relics of a beacon fire were found during the excavations.

The bridle-path which runs just past the earthworks is known as Lord Chatham's Walk, from the habit which that celebrated statesman formed of taking his periodical rides, upon the back of his favourite pony, round about this part of the Common. He is said to have had a particular dislike to be stared at, and when he saw any person approach, would often turn down the first lane or bye-way which happened to be near.

Flint Implements.

The large numbers of flint implements, both palæolithic and neolithic, which have been found by the writer in West Wickham, form a collection of considerable archæological value, and are important in the evidence they afford of the condition of the inhabitants of this district in the more remote periods of time. They are in fact the only remaining traces of the first two or three chapters of the history of West Wickham. The "palæolithic" period, illustrated by roughly-chipped axes, hatchets, and other flint implements, dates back to such an early period as to be entirely beyond the province of written history, and one can only roughly and vaguely speculate as to the immense number of years which separates that period from our own. In fact that early age may almost be considered to belong as much to the province of geology as to that of archæology; and, although nothing can be clearer to the unprejudiced student than that the implements of flint are the skilful and ingenious work of rational human beings, still, a considerable exercise of the imaginative power is necessary to fill up the details of the story of which they are the faint and indefinite, but unmistakable outlines. It was a fortunate circumstance which led the aborigines of our land to make a large number of their implements of hard, imperishable flint. Had such a substance as flint been unknown in England, or unsuitable for the manufacture of weapons and implements, much of the information we now possess as to the habits and mode of life of that primitive people must of necessity have remained unknown. A flint newly taken from its chalky bed is capable of being speedily and easily broken into a roughly cutting or piercing implement. The operations of a skilful workman engaged in squaring flints for the purpose of the builder, illustrate this in a remarkable manner. A few well-directed blows succeed in detaching flakes and splinters in any direction, and the block is shaped with great accuracy.

Among the ancient flint implements found at West Wickham one may notice many specimens of careful and practised handiwork; but perfect and well-shaped examples are comparatively rare. Most of them have been either spoiled in the making or discarded by the fastidious maker. This is not remarkable when one remembers the abundance of flints which naturally occur there. Some of the implements, too, after having been well shaped, have become accidentally broken, or perhaps broken in the using, and then rejected. Long-continued use, and repeated chippings and sharpenings, have rendered some unsuitable for further service. These, to us, are perhaps the most valuable relics, inasmuch as they afford strong evidence of the purpose and manner of their use.

Although it would be impossible in this place to give anything like a complete account of all the flint implements by which the searches of the writer from time to time at West Wickham have been rewarded, still some of the chief types may be enumerated.

Church Field has yielded a large number of palæolithic implements. The total number of finished implements which I have gathered from its surface is about fifty. In shape they resemble those implements which are generally known as "tongue-shaped" and "almond-shaped," and there are many intermediate forms. They vary in size, and, of course, in weight, but about a dozen are very nearly of the same size, shape, and weight. They are from two to three, or three and a-half inches in length. They are all stained and worn, but in different degrees. A small proportion are of much larger size and simpler manufacture, having been brought into the desired form by a few bold, skilful blows. They are remarkable as bearing marks of long-continued abrasion upon the angles and ridges. This is exactly the sort of wear which one would expect to arise from concussion with other large stones in the bed of a torrent arising from floods, or the bottom of a swollen river. So many of the Church Field implements are worn in this way that there is no doubt at all that at one period of their history they must have been subjected to some such abrading force. To such a degree are one or two specimens worn down, that it has been suggested that nothing short of sea-beach wear could account for their condition. But in sea wear one would expect the scratching and cutting of the sand and minute shingle to wear into the hollows as well as upon the angles and ridges, and of this there is no sign at all upon the implements of Church Field. In Carthouse Field, 403 feet above the sea-level, and about 100 feet above the bottom of the Church Field Valley, I found a palæolithic implement which seems never to have suffered any abrasion at all. It is much stained, and in other respects resembles the Church Field flints, but in its sharp, unworn character it is quite unlike them. Probably the high level on which it lay was out of reach of the floods and torrents which have written their history in such unmistakable and indelible characters upon the flints of Church Field. I found at Church Field an unworn flint core and several waste chips, a discovery which lends probability to the idea that dry land, where implements could be manufactured, was near at hand.

Scrapers and trimmed flints were not found in any great proportion at Church Field. The scrapers are of two kinds—those simply with a convex scraping edge, and double scrapers possessing one convex and one concave edge. Flakes are for the most part of a simple type, produced by blows from one direction, or, at least, before severance from the core; and some are large and much curved. Some chips are curved and twisted in a manner which indicates that they are nothing more than waste chips struck off and rejected by the implement maker.

Of drills or boring implements I have found no specimen, except one flint, which bears marks of having been heated at the point, and may have been used for burning rather than boring. Of course some of the larger pointed implements may have been used for boring.

From the manner in which many of the implements were formed, and the facility with which the chips were evidently struck off, it is probable that good flint, such as can be obtained only from the chalk itself, was employed in their manufacture. Such flint might have been easily obtained by digging into the chalk which forms the substratum of Church Field. There is no section exposed showing how deep the chalk actually is in Church Field, but in Lower Hackett's Orchard, and adjoining field, the chalk is close to the surface of the ground in one or two spots.

The palæolithic flint implements found in Church Field seem to be all more or less intimately associated with a stiff ochreous clay, which, from long-continued contact, has stained the flints with a rich yellow colour. The clay and stained flints are found in certain definite parts of the field, chiefly about the middle and south-western parts of it; they have evidently been naturally deposited there, on the western side of the little valley which runs through Church Field. A somewhat similar deposit of ferruginous clay and stained flints occurs in Stable Field, but hitherto I have not succeeded in finding any palæolithic flints in it. In the following fields at Rowes Farm, West Wickham, I have found palæolithic implements:—Church Field, Gates Green Field, Carthouse Field, Old Plantation, South Field, Moll Costen.

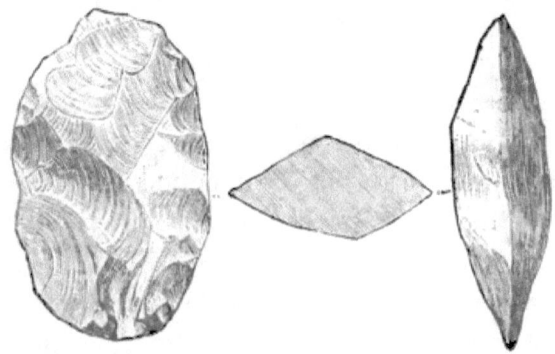

OVOID FLINT (PALÆOLITHIC), FOUND AT MOLL COSTEN.

Nearly every part of Rowes Farm has yielded neolithic implements in considerable numbers. In Moll Costen, formerly a wood, and now a fruit plantation, I have found more than three hundred, under such circumstances as to show conclusively that they were not only manufactured there, but that the place itself was the site of a village or group of human dwellings in neolithic times. The ancient hut floors were marked by groups of flint implements, broken and perfect, and by large pebbles thoroughly reddened by fire. That these spots were not merely chipping centres is indicated, firstly, by the fact that the scrapers and flakes found here have been much worn by use; secondly, the proportion of *domestic* implements is large; thirdly, the waste chips are not so numerous in proportion to the finished implements as one would expect to find in a place devoted solely to the manufacture of implements.

Particulars of the implements found are set forth at large in *Archæologia Cantiana*, vol. xiv., and *Proceedings of the Society of Antiquaries of London*, 2 S. xi., 161, *et seq.* Spear or javelin-heads, arrow-heads, and ground axes or celts are among the chief weapons found. Some of the arrow-heads are very beautifully finished pieces of work, and they are of the usual types, but one acutely-tapering, concave-based, and stemless specimen is a rare English type, and found more commonly in Ireland. The total number of ground celts, perfect and broken, is six. An unfinished javelin-head formed of tough honey-coloured flint is here represented. It is figured a little under the full size.

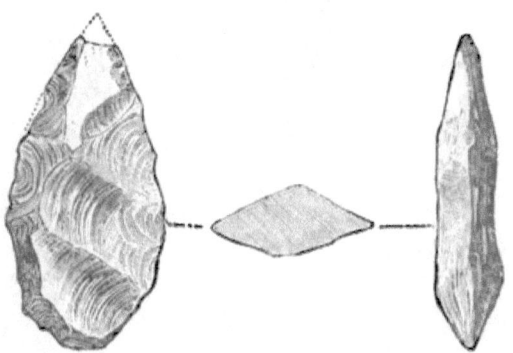

JAVELIN-HEAD (NEOLITHIC), FOUND AT MOLL COSTEN.

Some of the more minute implements, such as flakes, saws, and small scrapers, have been made with great skill and care. Borers, drills, arrow-scrapers, and hammer-stones are among the other implements found at Moll Costen.

The accompanying illustrations (page 186), show some of the characteristic forms. The three upper figures are scrapers, the two next, flakes, and that at the bottom of the plate is a drill or awl.

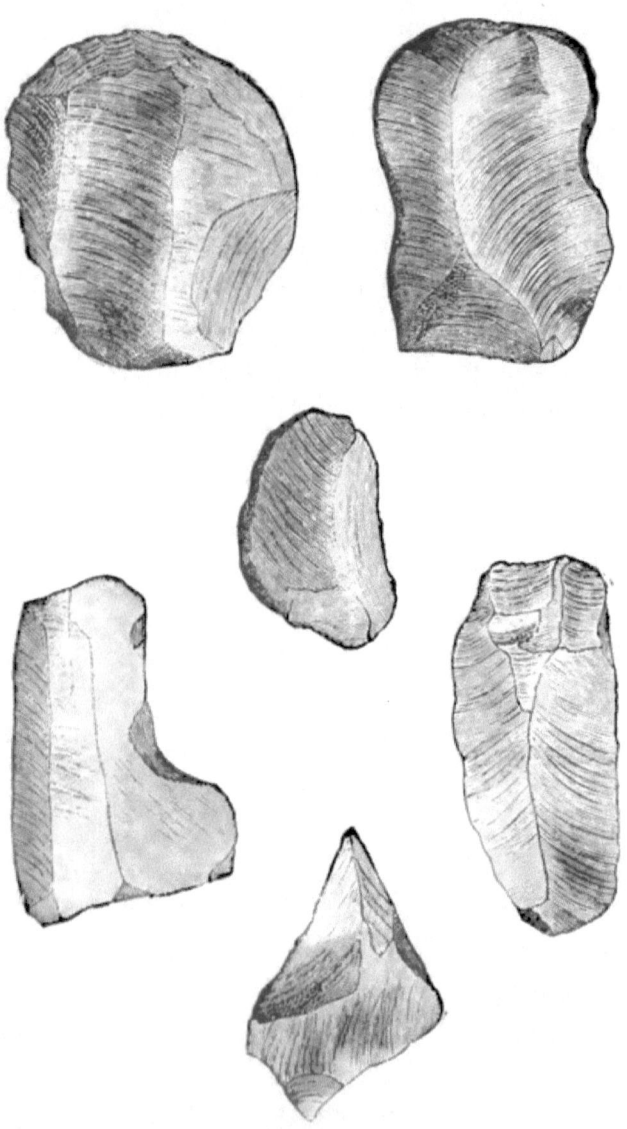

WROUGHT FLINTS FOUND AT WEST WICKHAM, IN KENT, 1880-1882.

Ancient Excavations.

A deep well-like pit of ancient appearance exists in Well Wood. A few years since it was about 48 feet deep, but when that measurement was made the lower part of the pit had been much filled up with rubbish. There is no doubt that it belongs to the class of subterranean excavations common in many parts of Kent, and known as dene-holes. A tradition affirms that there were formerly sixteen lateral galleries branching out from the bottom of the shaft. This tradition and the name Well Wood, evidently derived from the pit, are both in harmony with the theory that this is an ancient dene-hole. Further evidence in its support is to be found in the occurrence of traces of other subterranean excavations in about six places in the neighbouring fields. In a chalk pit close by Weights House there was, until the year 1881, a portion of another dene-hole, at a slighter depth below the surface. It consisted of two chambers carefully hollowed out of the chalk. Some years ago it was inhabited by an Irishman and his family, but in March 1881 the overhanging chalk and earth fell in and destroyed nearly all traces of it. From the antiquity and plan of the excavation it is probable that it formed part of a dene-hole much like those figured by Camden in his *Britannia* as existing at Tilbury, but of less depth below the surface of the ground.

INDEX.

	PAGE		PAGE
ADDINGTON, Anthony	112	Bromley market	9
Andrew, Sir John	100	,, market house	92
Angus, Jacob	129	,, monuments	75
Antoninus, Pius, coin of	3	,, Norman pottery	4
Archdeacon's Well, Keston	134	,, Palace	10
Atterbury, Francis	20	,, ,, Bishop's, at	13
		,, parish umbrella	86
BASTON manor	119-121	,, prehistoric antiquities	3
Beeby, W. T.	7, 10, 11, 12, 35, 57	,, rectors and vicars	83
Beechfield, Roman pottery	4	,, rectory	85
Belknap, Sir Robert	149, 162	,, tokens	91
Blackbrook manor	8, 35	Bruce, James	111
Bodenham, Jane	73	"Bull Inn," Bromley	90
Bradgate, Elizabeth	105		
Bread and Ale, Assize of	8	CÆSAR's Well, Keston	135
Brent, Cecil	3	Camden, William	178
Bromley, ancient names	3	Cator, John Farnaby. See Lennard	
,, bells	67	Clarke, Christopher	150
,, benefactions	51, 80	Chatham's (Lord) Walk	179
,, brasses	71	Cleaver, Ann	107
,, church	55	,, Jane	107
,, ,, door	70	Colchester, Duncomb	149
,, ,, goods	62	Coltman, W. J.	106
,, ,, plate	65	Coney Hall Farm	178
,, college	43	Copledike, John	175
,, ,, trustees	47	Corner, G. R.	147, 150
,, Easter sepulchre	60	Chatham, Earl of	113, 116-118
,, extent of	3	Child, Coles	8, 10
,, fair	9	Croker, T. C.	151
,, font	58	Cumberledge, S. A.	106
,, funereal garland	86		
,, Hill Place	38	DAVIDSON, Robert	110
,, manor	5	Devon, Harriet, Countess of	164

INDEX.

	PAGE
Dolben, John	14
ELIOTT, G. A.	165
Elmfield Road, Bromley, pottery at	3
FARNABY, Sir C. F.	165
,, Sir J.	176
Fawkes, Francis	114
Fenton, William	107
Fitzhubert, Adam	173
Franc-pledge	8
Funereal garland	4
GARRET, Robert	101
Gates Green, Roman tiles	153
"George Inn," Hayes	97
Gibbs, Sir Vicary	107
Glynne, Sir S., on Bromley Church	57, 58
,, on West Wickham Church	159
Green, Jane	150
HANDFORD, John	103
Harriet, Countess of Devon	164
Hawkesworth, John	78
Hayes, ancient name	97
,, bells	99
,, brasses	100
,, church	97
,, ,, goods	107
,, common	122
,, monuments	103
,, parish register	110
,, Place	115
,, Roman tiles, &c.	153
Henche, Walter de	71
Heydon, Sir Christopher	175
,, Henry	175
,, Sir John	175
,, Sir William	175
Heygge, John	101
Hinton, John	106
,, Sarah	106

	PAGE
Hoare, John	102
Hobbes, Margaret	163
Hodgson, E. A.	147
,, James	147
,, Jane	147
,, John	147
Holwood Camp	136
,, House	139
Huntingfield, Peter de	174
,, Sir Walter de	162, 174
ILOTT, J. W.	4
JACOB'S Well, Hayes	129
James II.	91
Johnson, Mrs S.	75
KAY, Alice	149
Kelk, Peter	82
Kempe, A. J.	151
Keston, ancient name	133
,, trees	141
,, bells	145
,, church	142
,, ,, goods	145
,, communion table	146
,, Mark	133, 147, 157
,, Roman lamp	153
,, windmills	133
King, John	73
Kirkpatrick, George	148
Knight, Thomas	36
LACER, Richard	72
Lang, John	161
Leland, John, on West Wickham Church	159
Lennard, John	175
,, Sir J. F.	176
,, Sir Samuel	164, 175
,, Sir Stephen	175
London, Tower of	22
Long, Rt. Hon. Chas.	39

INDEX.

	PAGE
Mahon, Charles Viscount	113
Maunsell, John	74
Monk, Elizabeth	79
Mot, Robert	99
Mumford, John	115
Nichols, W. J.	126
Osteler, John	100, 162
Parker, Prof., on Keston Church	144
Payne, G. H.	3
Pearce, Zachary	76
Perch, Elizabeth	148
" Judith	148
Pickhurst manor	119
Pitt, John, 2nd Earl of Chatham	112
" William	112, 116
Raleigh, Sir Walter	177
Ravensbourne	135
Ravenscroft, Bromley	90
Reeve, Ann	105
Reynolds, Thomas	25
Rowes Farm, Roman pottery	153
St Blaze's Well, Bromley	24
Scott, Ann	105
" Edmund	104
" Sir Edmund	106
" John	104
" Sir Stephen	103
Scrope, Richard	175
Sheppard College	51
Simpson's manor	8
Simpson's Place	28
Smith, Jane	148
" J. A.	107
Sprat, Thomas	15
Squerie, Thomas	175
Stanhope, Lady H. L.	113
Stockton, John	161
Suling	5

	PAGE
Sundridge manor	8, 33
Thornhill, Richard	36, 72
Thorp, William de	161
Till, John	106, 114
Tokens, Bromley	91
Toots Wood, earthworks	126-129
Trail, C., G. M., J., J. M., J. S., and W. B. T.	107
Tuppingdens (Tuppington Farm)	36
Waller, J. G.	61, 162, 167-8
Walwyn, John	106
War Bank, Keston	150
" funeral urn	151
" Roman coins	153
Warner, John	13
Well Wood	187
Wesley, John	94
West, Gilbert	165
West Wickham, ancient name	157
" " excavations	187
" bells	166
" charities	172
" church	157
" " field	181
" " goods	170
" Court	173
" earthworks	178
" flint implements	180
" lich-gate	173
" Moll Costen	184
" monuments	160
" painted glass	167
" registers	172
" roodscreen	165
Whately, E. M.	107
" William	107
Widmore	93
Withernam	9
Yarwood, Ann	106
" Charles	106

www.ingramcontent.com/pod-product-compliance
Lightning Source LLC
Chambersburg PA
CBHW021733220426
43662CB00008B/827